Creating the Buy-in Magnet

Creating the Buy-in Magnet

Leading Cross-Functional Teams to Achieve Extraordinary Success

Douglas W. Chapman
MBA, BSBA

First Printing: 2018

ISBN 978-0-692-15409-0

This book is dedicated to the breadwinners who routinely get up each morning and head to their places of work. They are the unsung heroes that labor week-in and week-out to put food on the table for their families. They put their self-interests aside to provide the best possible future for the generation to come. Their spouses and significant others also deserve recognition for the encouragement and support they provide especially during the down times of an ever-changing business world.

CONTENTS

FIGURES

TABLES

Preface

This is a business book about leadership. In the business world, the term *leadership* conjures up images of CEOs, COOs, Directors, Vice Presidents and others perched in the higher echelons of their company's organization. This book is not about them. Rather, it is intended as a guide for individual contributors who are tasked with the enormous challenges of getting difficult things done using resources that are not under their direct control.

Some have called this *Leadership without Authority* and it is a common concept discussed in many MBA programs. Effective leadership of this type is arguably more difficult to achieve than having a team of subordinates whose careers depend on their leader's approval and yearly performance reviews. Individual contributors can only rely on their skill and interpersonal influence to render positive outcomes. It's not easy but it is achievable if you know how to execute.

I spent the past four decades of my career in the Information Technology industry. I've held numerous leadership positions as VP, Director and Manager with direct reports and also as an individual contributor leading cross-functional teams. In some instances, my team developed large-scale IT solutions that were deployed internally to run my company's business. In others, I led teams that developed IT solutions for sale to external customers. In almost all of the cases, the goals were very aggressive. I felt enormous pressure to deliver. At times, I seriously wondered whether my job might be in jeopardy if I failed.

Some of the tasks that were given to me were previously attempted by others but resulted in failure. At first, I was apprehensive when faced with the possibility of restarting a previously failed project. Why would my efforts have a different outcome? How could I be successful when others have failed? However, management's expectations were clear: "You are now at bat and it is time for you to swing at the knuckleball. We'd like to see you hit a home run." I sweated it out but never lost focus.

Fortunately for me, I was able to connect and more than my fair share of balls went over the fences.

I have frequently been asked how I have been able to achieve successful business outcomes when others have tried and failed. As an individual contributor, many of my accomplishments resulted in tens of millions of dollars being added to the top and bottom lines of the business. Although my usual response when questioned was "it's all in the preparation", I never really had the opportunity to fully explain my method and how it can be effectively utilized by others.

That is the subject of this book. It is a practical guide for the individual contributor who is faced with a difficult business objective that requires near-flawless execution by a team. It's about leadership and goes far beyond project management as you will find out. By following the framework outlined in the following chapters, I am confident that you too can lead cross-functional teams to achieve extraordinary results. You will find that it is an iterative process that builds on itself and strengthens as you progress along the path. As a result, your value to your organization will rise precipitously and your influence and skills will always be in high demand.

Doug Chapman

Chapter 1: Introduction

Has your boss ever asked to you perform a task or reach a goal that you felt was too aggressive or unattainable? Lofty goals are many times confused with the unattainable and are deflected, put aside or simply swept "under the rug." When faced with this situation human nature causes energy to be expended in building a case for *can't do it* rather than *can do it*.

You may or may not be old enough to remember John F. Kennedy's speech to the Joint Session of Congress in which he said:

> *I believe that this nation should commit itself to achieving the goal, before this decade is out, of landing a man on the moon and returning him safely to the earth.*

> -JFK, Man on the Moon Speech, Joint Session of Congress May 25, 1961

In this speech, the President was asking Congress to provide funding for this extremely ambitious and risky goal. It is without a doubt one of the most audacious and far-reaching proposals of the Twentieth Century. It was met with skepticism by many. For them, it seemed impossible to achieve and exorbitantly expensive.

For the rest of the Nation, it captured their imagination. They were inspired but there were also lingering doubts if this was truly possible. It had never been done before and it was very risky. However, they were committed. For them, the only way forward for the Nation was to provide the funding for this historic project that later became known as "The Moon Shot." What followed was a decade of dedication, planning, experimentation, courage and heroics.

On July 20, 1969, the World was astonished as it heard a crackly statement come across the airways that said:

> *That's one small step for man, one giant leap for mankind.*

-Neil Armstrong, NASA astronaut, upon first stepping onto the Moon's surface.

Neil Armstrong and his crew safely returned to Earth and the seemly impossible mission was accomplished.

Although this is an extreme example, I believe many of us can relate to the times in our careers when we were asked to take responsibility for what we perceived as a "Moon Shot." How did we cope with this? Did we reject it as impossible? Sadly, many achievable opportunities find themselves on the scrap heap given this attitude. Many people have become adept at crafting convincing reasons why not to pursue a project. They may not get fired over it and their careers continue to plod along leaving behind a wake of mediocrity.

We can do better than that. Just think about the lost opportunity. What if the seemingly impossible goal could be achieved? How much value does it hold for your organization? If you were asked to lead it, there probably is significant value in it. If there is enough value for your organization, management will most likely pony up the resources you feel are necessary to get the job done. Part of your responsibility will be to do the preparation necessary to make this happen. This book will show you how. If you are leading the effort and deliver successful results, your value to your organization will assume a steep trajectory.

Let's take a moment to clear up any confusion regarding the distinction between the leadership I am describing and *project management*. Most business tasks are commonly referred to as projects. They may last a few weeks, a few months or even longer. A project manager is usually assigned to track the project to its completion. This includes accounting for budgets, hours spent, and other resources consumed while proceeding along the critical path to the goal. A key responsibility of the project manager is to alert management when the project is at risk of delay or veers off course. Although there is some overlap, that is not what this book is about. There is no shortage of books already written on effective project management and its many frameworks and methodologies.

The project manager usually has resources assigned to the project prior to taking ownership. His time is spent tracking progress and scheduling status meetings. He periodically reports the status of the project to management regarding how it is proceeding. The project manager's key responsibility is to keep the project moving ahead by diligently tracking and reporting any discrepancies with the plan. If deviations are reported, he also provides recommendations to management for correction.

On the other hand, one tasked with assembling and leading a team who is not under one's direct control has a much greater span of responsibilities than the project manager and the "lift" is much heavier. This type of leader starts much earlier in the process. She takes a concept or idea and moves it all the way along the path to fruition. In fact, the leader may even have a project manager assigned to her project as a resource. That would be up to the leader to determine.

So, what additional responsibilities does the leader have that the project manager does not? As I mentioned earlier, the leader is usually asked by management to achieve a particularly difficult goal. Because of its complexity and challenging aspects, it would be impossible for one person alone to achieve the goal. Think of The Moon Shot and how many thousands of people of varying disciplines were involved. Neil Armstrong alone could never have placed himself on the Moon without the help of a very large and talented team of dedicated individuals.

The leader takes the initial idea or goal given to her by management and first studies its feasibility. Can this be accomplished given the right resources and discipline? Is the goal just exceedingly aggressive or would it truly be impossible or impractical to accomplish?

The old medieval practice of alchemy is a good example of a goal that was impossible to reach. For many years alchemists tried to convert base metals into gold. Imagine having a secret process for manufacturing gold! What a huge payoff this would create, at least in the short-term. The alchemists were never successful reaching this goal and the enormous energy they put into its discovery eventually died. If anyone every asks you to convert metal into gold, politely say "no" and suggest a more productive pursuit!

Another example of an unreachable goal is the so-called Fountain of Youth. For years ambitious explorers sought the elixir for everlasting life on Earth. Like alchemy, the rewards were perceived to be so great that enormous energy and treasure were expended on this ill-fated quest. Although modern medicine has extended man's lifetime by several decades, no one has yet found a way to make a man or woman live forever on Earth. However, all was not lost. This concept has made for some entertaining adventures portrayed in Hollywood movies.

These two examples illustrate the difference between impossible goals and lofty goals. Putting a man on the moon was a lofty goal but, given the right resources, funding and energy it was proven achievable on that summer day in 1969. The leader is concerned with the distinction between *impossible* and *lofty*. She doesn't want to waste time or resources chasing the impossible. She must take all relevant factors into consideration in the qualification process. To be credible, her findings must be substantiated by a thorough analysis and concrete facts to back up her conclusion. Once this is done the leader will reach an informed decision whether to proceed along the path to the goal or end the effort.

If the leader decides to proceed, there is still much to be done before the task is actually undertaken. There are other obstacles along the way that must be overcome. For example, how much will it cost the organization to achieve the goal? Depending on the aggressiveness or loftiness of the goal, the path may be very costly both in dollars and human resources. What are the real benefits to the organization once the goal is reached? Do the benefits outweigh the costs and if so, by how much? Are there ancillary or intangible benefits to be realized beyond the financial return on investment? How compelling is the argument to proceed? These questions must be answered with credibility. It is the leader's responsibility to do the analysis and reach a rational conclusion that stakeholders can appreciate and buy into.

This book will show you how to approach an ambitious or *stretch* goal and successfully take it from start to finish. Your team will get you there but you will be the one at the helm. Like a ship's captain, you will need to know the route, how to skillfully navigate the sometimes treacherous "waters" and what to avoid. You will determine what is important and what to filter out. Like the repeated successes of the Moon Shots that followed the first, upon reaching your goal how can you prepare the next one? All the steps and techniques necessary to successfully accomplish this and more will be discussed in the chapters ahead.

Let's get started!

Chapter 2: Planning for Success

When our kids were growing up, my wife and I always stressed that they should put their best efforts into their studies and extracurricular school activities. By doing this, they would more fully develop their skills and talents and those would come in handy later in life. Our message was that, by putting in the extra effort on the front-end during their young lives, what would come later would be much more fulfilling.

Consider someone who has the potential to develop talent or skills but never does. You probably remember some of them in high school. Although some of these folks found their passion and became very successful later in life, others struggled to maintain an even modest lifestyle. The unfortunate ones found themselves having to work two or three jobs just to make ends meet. This put a limit on the quality time they could spend with their families. If they had only prepared a little more on the front-end – learned a skill or took education more seriously – their later lives may have been much easier and more fulfilling.

Of course, this isn't limited to monetary rewards and success can take many forms. Take the example of a fifth-grade boy who was presented with the opportunity to take piano lessons. Due to apathy, he never really practiced and did just enough to get by. Later in life he wished he had learned how to play piano for the pure enjoyment of it. He later regretted the inaction he had taken as a young boy. Now, having a full-time job and a family to support, he found it exceedingly difficult to find the time and learn how to play this rewarding instrument. If he had only put more effort in on the front-end, he probably would now be playing the songs he enjoys hearing others play. I know from experience. I was that boy.

I think we can learn from these examples. In life, missed opportunity and inaction due to apathy or lack of effort in one area can always be balanced with success in others. The business world is not as forgiving. We are judged by how successful we are in doing our jobs. We are recognized by how well we execute. After all, we are being paid for it. Our performance is usually viewed in a narrow or singular way because it is based on our success with very specific tasks. To execute at the highest level of our abilities, we must plan accordingly.

Disciplined planning effort on the front-end of a complex project will, without a doubt make the execution during the later phases much easier. In fact, for these ambitious types of projects, careful planning is a necessity and can easily make the difference between success and failure. As I mentioned earlier in the book, my response when questioned about my own success, I usually answered with "it's all in the planning." Although that terse answer was a bit flippant, it underscores the importance of this phase of the endeavor.

Every task or successful business undertaking starts with a need. "We need to increase sales, we need to develop a product solution that will sell briskly in our market segment, we need to increase customer satisfaction, we need to implement a Cloud-based human resource system" are a few common examples.

The need must also be real. Many years ago, a colleague of mine joined a venture capital backed startup company that was intent on manufacturing and selling single user computer workstations for $100,000 per unit. Although the technology was powerful and very advanced, there simply wasn't a market for it. Who would spend $100,000 for a computer that only one person could use at a time? When the company eventually filed for bankruptcy, he described their efforts as "the greatest solution to a problem that never existed." The need was not real. As the saying goes, "hindsight is always 20/20", especially with high-risk startups. However, I hope I am not being too unfair by wondering whether enough planning had been done on the front-end of this venture with a thorough market analysis.

The need is conceptualized in the Idea activity of the Planning Phase. It is then fully vetted in the Feasibility activity. The four major activities in the Planning Phase are shown in Figure 1 below.

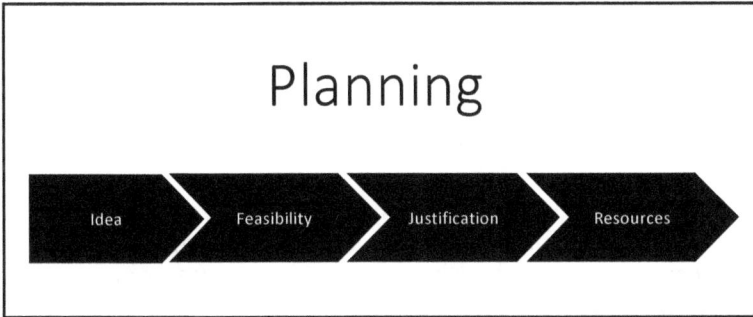

Figure 1 - Planning Phase

Idea

Business tasks can be broken into three fundamental elements: *what, when and how*. It is up to the leader to fully understand all three elements culminating with a laser focus on the *how*. The *how* as we will find out later is a compelling, documented description of what is needed to get to the goal in the required period of time.

Every ambitious task starts with a seed idea. It may be very specific or it may be vague. This phase deals with "what" needs to be accomplished. JFK's words regarding The Moon Shot were very specific. He described:

the *what*:

> *landing a man on the moon and returning him safely to the earth*

and also, the *when*:

> *before this decade is out*

Note that JFK never discussed the *how*. He left that up to the team.

Consider a business executive's statement "we need to increase our revenues and margins in the Healthcare segment of our business." The *what* is very clear. Obviously, the solution would be to increase sales. However, the *when* and *how* are not defined.

There are many options and missing information at this point. Should the salesforce be trained so it can be more productive? Should more salespeople be hired? Does the company have something to sell that customers want? What are the expectations for when the goal is met and is paying off?

You as the leader and prospective solution provider need to analyze and identify the possible options and their potential outcomes. There may be several. Look for input from others where you can. The possibilities are identified in the Idea activity. At this point, they are only ideas and are not fully rationalized. This is the "notes written on the back of the napkin" stage. The analysis will occur in later stages of the planning. You could think of it as a disciplined brainstorming session.

Remember to document your ideas. If you used a "back of the napkin" approach, make sure you transpose your thoughts to a permanent record on your computer or loose-leaf binder. You may need to go back later and refer to an alternative approach after finding the first choice is not feasible. Thorough documentation also provides proof and credibility regarding your influence in the organization. This is critical and will be discussed later in detail.

Here are a few examples of possible solutions to the business executive's request to increase revenues and margins. You may be able to think of more.

1. Hire more salespeople.
2. Train existing sales force to become more productive.
3. Provide additional incentives to sales force.
4. Build a new product that has appeal to an existing market segment.
5. Strengthen marketing efforts.

6. Expand into new, untapped markets.
7. Increase the average transaction size.
8. Expand sales channels through partners.

Remember, these are just ideas. The vetting will occur in the Feasibility activity which is discussed next.

Feasibility

The Feasibility activity is broken down into two parts:

1. Qualifying and
2. Quantifying

Qualifying deals with whether the goal is achievable. Quantifying deals with how much it will cost.

Qualifying

Qualifying is where you look at all options identified in the Idea activity. This is where you separate "alchemy" from a "Moon Shot." With alchemy, no matter how much time and effort are spent, the chances of manufacturing gold are close to or at zero. That option should be pulled off the table of further consideration as it would be a waste of time and resources. This is known as *qualifying out.*

With the Moon Shot, experts concluded that it could be achievable if enough time, effort and money were dedicated to the project. At this point those resources weren't quantified but it was qualified as being possible. That is the main objective of this part of the Feasibility activity – to identify those options that are achievable.

A common idiom is "Anything is possible if you throw enough money at it." This isn't a correct statement. Has anyone ever invented a gravity shield, a device that would shield the gravitational pull of the Earth and enable you to float in mid-air? This was attempted in the first half of the 20th Century with considerable funding. Sadly, it never culminated in a success. A better statement would be "Many things are possible if you put enough time, energy and funding into it."

Once you have eliminated the options from your list that you feel are unachievable or unrealistic, you are ready to make a decision. Pick the option that you feel has the greatest chance of success while providing the greatest benefit to your company. Your decision will be based on preliminary conversations with colleagues and some degree of gut feel. It will later need further refinement.

Once you have selected an option, you are ready to move on to the next activity which is quantifying the effort and resources needed to achieve the goal. As you gather more information, your decision to move forward may be reinforced or possibly rejected.

Quantifying

Quantifying deals with the question "How much will it cost and how long will it take?" This can include any number of expenses depending on what your task entails. To illustrate this, let's walk through a very simple example.

In a recent company meeting, a senior sales executive emphasized that increased sales and margins are critical to maintain the momentum of the company's current growth trajectory. He stated that it is not just the responsibility of the sales force to make this happen. Everyone in the company is responsible and should contribute through their respective job functions. In short "Everyone should have an oar in the water and they should be pulling hard."

Imagine you work for a company that sells a variety of computer equipment that includes servers, networking and storage. Your company partners with various Independent Software Vendors (ISV's) who supply application software to run on your equipment. Unfortunately, your company has been losing sales to the competition in the Healthcare market. Your company does not have an integrated and tested Electronic Medical Records

24

(EMR) solution. Healthcare customers such as hospitals will not buy an integrated IT solution from a vendor that has not been fully tested. This includes certification by the EMR ISV as being compliant with their performance requirements. Potential customers feel that an untested and un-certified solution is too risky and are unwilling to bet their business on it.

Your manager approaches you and asks if you can remedy this deficiency. She states that the Healthcare market is growing rapidly and is a strategic market segment for your company. The competition has a certified solution and is signing up customers at an alarming rate. Without a viable solution within the next six months, your company risks being sidelined and this market opportunity will be lost.

You find out later that certification testing was previously attempted but failed. Upon further analysis, you find that the failed attempt was staffed by competent engineers but lacked disciplined leadership. This resulted in a sporadic and haphazard approach. Due to this unfortunate event, future attempts were met with skepticism and the project languished.

To add to the challenge, you recognize that this goal is a significant stretch because *the necessary resources are not under your direct control*. They are located in other organizational departments within your company. To be successful you will need to assemble, motivate and lead a cross-functional team over the finish line.

Know Your Target

Many projects fail because the question "How is success defined?" is too often never asked. Other times it is asked but the answer is vague. You must understand exactly what the goal is and how success is measured. It's extraordinarily difficult to hit a target that hasn't been identified. Woe be to the deer hunter who indiscriminately fires his rifle into the woods in hopes of hitting a deer. He may get lucky and shoot one but it is highly improbable. Worse, he may shoot another hunter which most certainly would derail his plans for having venison for dinner that evening!

Although you may be eager to get started, don't fall into the *ready, fire, aim* trap. You can burn through a lot of resources leading a team in a vague or wrong direction. This is a recipe for disaster. Know your target and know how success is measured. It's the metric that will define your success.

After meeting with the EMR ISV Partner Alliance Manager you find that his company's certification requirements are based on infrastructure performance. Specifically, a six-server configuration using a single storage array must be capable of performing a minimum of 5,000 transactions per second. It's a definitive measure of success or failure. The EMR ISV will provide the software to produce the load and measure the transaction level. You now know exactly what the goal is. Armed with this metric, you would like to further dial in on the feasibility with the help of an expert. You set up a meeting with a senior performance engineer who is familiar with the infrastructure capabilities. After some analysis, he feels the goal is a stretch but is probably achievable.

At this point, you feel the goal of producing a viable Healthcare EMR infrastructure solution is within reach. However, you don't know how much it will cost. Is it really worth it? It's time to sharpen your pencil and make a list of all the resources that will be required. You don't need to be specific as to who or what should be involved. You only need to identify roles and generic resources. Specific names and organizational groups will be identified later in the Resources activity. Remember, you are still in the Feasibility activity and are only dealing with estimates.

After speaking with several experienced engineers, product managers and specialists, you arrive at the following list of resources needed to get this done within a six-month period:

- Performance Engineer
- Lab Technician
- Systems Engineer

- Product Manager
- Test Lab

You may also want to include a project manager who may be able to supply a *Level of Effort* with cost estimates and durations for each role. That will make your job of estimating the overall project cost much easier. The project manager can also assume the responsibility of tracking this task over its lifetime. If a project manager is not involved you'll have to come up with your own estimates and do your own tracking. For the sake of simplified illustration, I have not included one in this example.

Sharpen Your Pencil

An electronic spreadsheet such as Microsoft Excel will be an invaluable tool for this analysis. You can also perform the calculations with a calculator and paper and pencil but make sure you have a big pink eraser handy. You will probably make several changes before you are satisfied with the final estimates.

Human Resource Costs

Start by making assumptions regarding the human resource costs. Find out what an average yearly base salary rate is for each role. Your human resources department may be reluctant to give you this information so you may have to get estimates from peers or online sources. The yearly salary is usually uplifted by a factor such at 30% (yearly salary x 1.30) to account for company benefits paid to the individual. You can then arrive at an hourly rate for each role by dividing the total yearly compensation by the number of hours in your work year. Your mileage may vary.

For this example, let's make some assumptions and perform some elementary calculations so we can arrive at the uplifted hourly cost for each of these roles as shown in Table 1 below.

Role	Yearly Salary	Total Yearly Compensation	Hourly Rate
Performance Engineer	$100,000	$130,000	$65.00
Lab Technician	$50,000	$65,000	$32.50
Systems Engineer	$75,000	$97,500	$48.75
Product Manager	$100,000	$130,000	$65.00
Leader (that's you)	$100,000	$130,000	$65.00
Salary Uplift for Benefits Compensation	30%		
Working Hours per 50 Week Year	2,000		

Table 1 - Hourly Rates

The next step is to estimate how many hours are required by each role for their involvement in the project. All roles are rarely busy over the entire span of the project. For example, the lab technician may only be needed for the set up and break down of the equipment at the beginning and end of the project. Again, a good project manager can help you with these estimates or even make them for you. For our example, some rough estimates are included in Table 2 below.

Role	Month						Hours by Role
	1	2	3	4	5	6	
Performance Engineer		40	40	40	40		160
Lab Technician	80					20	100
Systems Engineer	80	40	40	40	40		240
Product Manager	8						8
Leader (that's you)	160	40	40	40	40	160	480

Table 2 - Hours by Role

Given your estimates so far, it is now easy to calculate the total estimated human resource costs of the project. Simply multiply the hours required by each role by their hourly rate and total them up as shown in Table 3.

Role	Yearly Salary	Total Yearly Compensation	Hourly Rate	Hours Required	HR Cost
Performance Engineer	$100,000	$130,000	$65.00	160	$10,400
Lab Technician	$50,000	$65,000	$32.50	100	$3,250
Systems Engineer	$75,000	$97,500	$48.75	240	$11,700
Product Manager	$100,000	$130,000	$65.00	8	$520
Leader (that's you)	$100,000	$130,000	$65.00	480	$31,200
Salary Uplift for Benefits Compensation	30%				
Working Hours per 50 Week Year	2,000			Total HR Cost	$57,070

Table 3 - HR Cost

Lab Costs

You also indicated in your initial analysis that you'll need a computer lab to complete this testing. You can break this down into two major cost categories:

1. Real Estate
2. Equipment

We could have included other categories of expenses such as power and cooling costs but, to keep it simple let's just go with the above two categories.

First, work on the real estate estimate and decide on how large a lab space you'll need. For the purpose of this exercise, let's assume a 15-foot by 15-foot area is sufficient. Next, you'll need to figure the cost to your company for the space. After all, rent is not free. You can usually get this from your accounting or finance department. Let's assume $40 per square foot per month is the cost. We now have enough information to calculate the real estate costs for the duration of the project as shown in Table 4.

Lab Length (feet)	Lab Width (feet)	Lab Area (square feet)	Monthly Cost Per Square Foot	Total Monthly Cost	Project Duration (months)	Total Lab Real Estate Cost
15	15	225	$40	$9,000	6	$54,000

Table 4 - Real Estate Cost

Next, we will estimate equipment costs. Start by developing a list of the equipment that is required for the project. For our example, assume the following equipment will be needed:

- 6 – Intel Servers running Microsoft server
- 2 – Network Switches to connect the servers to the storage array
- 1 – Storage Array

A yearly or monthly cost for each equipment type can usually be obtained from your accounting or finance department. A lab manager may also be a good source. These figures are typically based on actual amortization schedules or rent costs. We are assuming the EMR application software will be provided free of charge by the EMR ISV partner company. Table 5 below shows an estimate of the equipment cost.

Equipment Type	Quantity	Monthly Cost	Total Equipment Cost
Servers	6	$75	$450
Network Switches	2	$50	$300
Storage Array	1	$1,500	$9,000
Project Duration (months)	6	Total Cost	$9,750

Table 5 - Equipment Cost

Total lab costs can now be calculated and summarized as shown in Table 6 below.

Expense Type	Lab Cost
Real Estate	$54,000
Equipment	$9,750
Total Lab Cost	$63,750

Table 6 - Lab Cost

Project Cost

Now that we have made rational estimates of all costs, we can summarize the total cost of the project as shown in Table 7 below.

Expense Type	Project Cost
Human Resources	$57,070
Lab	$63,750
Total Project Cost	$120,820

Table 7 - Project Cost

At this point you may be wondering whether this book is about leadership or financial analysis. Please bear with me and rest assured that crunching the numbers as we have done is necessary for effective leadership of this type. You are in the process of building a compelling case that will be communicated to the stakeholders in your organization. You will need to demonstrate strong credibility to gain their support for securing the required resources.

Remember, you will be relying on resources that are not under your direct control. Credibility is paramount in effective leadership and we will be discussing it in more detail in later chapters. For now, let's continue building our case.

In the Feasibility activity we have determined that a) the goal is probably achievable and b) we have an estimate for what resources are needed and how much they will cost. What we don't know is whether $120,820 is worth investing in this project. We will determine that in the Justification activity which is discussed in the next section.

Justification

The Justification activity answers the question "Given the costs, is this goal worth pursuing?" To get a handle on this, we must first determine what a successful outcome means for our company. What is the benefit? Can we quantify it or is it less tangible?

If we determine that reaching our goal would increase sales revenue for our company by $1M per year, we have a quantifiable and tangible benefit. If we think we could significantly increase customer satisfaction, the benefits may be harder to quantify and less tangible. Would we experience increased repeat sales from more satisfied customers? If so, can this be quantified? Perhaps increased customer satisfaction would also enhance our industry brand image, which is still a benefit but much harder to quantify.

Our goal in this activity is to identify the primary benefit or benefits associated with achieving our goal. The basis for a solid justification rests with how tangible and quantifiable the benefit is and how credible our estimates are. Once we make this determination we can make a few simple calculations to arrive at a *go* or *no-go* decision whether we should continue down this path.

Keep in mind that as we continue moving through the Planning phase, we are also building credibility. This will be critical for success in subsequent stages of this process. One of the most important aspects of leadership is the ability to influence others in your organization in support of the goal. Without credibility, your efforts will be met with resistance or completely ignored.

Let's take a closer look at Justification through a simple example.

When I was seventeen years old, I had a lawn mowing business that provided some spending money and a small contribution to my college savings. As a young entrepreneur, I was surprised to find how many of my neighbors were eager to employ my services. Perhaps the price was right or maybe they just thought supporting my fledgling enterprise was for a good cause. Either way, I found I had more demand for my work that I could fulfill given the limited hours I could devote to it after school and during summer vacations.

I started out using my parents old non-motorized push mower and their well-worn lawn sweeper for removing the clippings. Although this old equipment worked well, my lawn mowing efforts were slow and labor intensive.

After the first few weeks of hard work a friend offered to sell me his used Briggs and Stratton 25-inch-wide power mower for $50. It blew a moderate amount of blue smoke and was a bit hard starting. However, after a few hard pulls on the starter cord and some fiddling with the choke the mower would start and seemed to run and cut well. It also came with a side bag to catch the grass clippings. Given the wider cutting swath and the bag to catch the clippings, I thought I could cut each lawn much faster using just a single pass. The downside was the $50 he wanted for the mower. This represented a small fortune for me at the time.

How could I justify taking $50 of my hard-earned savings to purchase this mower? Should I spend the $50 to purchase the power mower or continue using the labor-intensive push mower and lawn sweeper combination? Can I justify the purchase?

To start, I identified the primary benefit. I figured with the power mower I could cut lawns at twice the rate since the mowing and bagging could be done in a single pass, not two passes as required with the push mower and sweeper combination. Since I had plenty of demand for my services, I could cut twice the number of lawns in the same period of time. Now that I quantified the benefit, I could do justification analysis.

With the push mower and sweeper, I would typically cut one lawn each weekday after school, charging an average $10 per lawn. I had other activities on the weekend so I didn't mow on those two days.

Payback Period

My currently weekly sales revenue was 5 days x 1 lawn per day x $10 per lawn = $50 per week. It was clear to me that the mower would cost me a week's pay. At first it seemed like too much to part with until I realized that the payback period was very short for this investment.

The Payback Period is defined as:

> *The time required for the amount invested in to be repaid by the net cash flow generated by the investment.*

The Payback Period is calculated as follows:

$$\frac{Cost\ of\ the\ Investment}{Periodic\ Cash\ Flow\ Generated\ by\ the\ Investment}$$

Remember that I estimated I could cut twice the number of lawns in the same period of time with the power mower. I would be making $10 more per day as a result of the increased productivity using the power mower. Since my work week consisted of five days, I would make $50 more per week.

$$\frac{\$50\ Cost\ of\ Mower}{\$50\ Extra\ Cash\ Per\ Week} = 1\ week\ payback\ period$$

I reaffirmed that the mower would "pay for itself" in just one week. Furthermore, it would continue to generate $50 per week after that. Over a six-month lawn cutting season, the power mower could provide an extra $1,200. Since I paid $50 for the mower, I needed to subtract that to arrive at the net extra cash generated from this investment:

> (6-month season x 4 weeks per month x $50 extra per week from power mower) - $50 cost of mower = $1,150 net extra per season

This can be expressed graphically as show in Figure 2. Note that the intersection of the two lines represents the Payback Period of 1 week. That is the point where the mower was "paid off" and the incremental cash beyond that point in time went directly into my pocket for college.

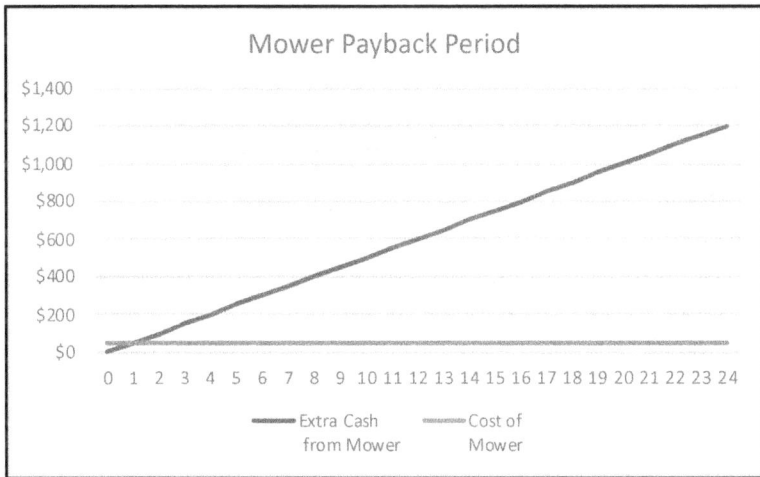

Figure 2 - Mower Payback Period

It seemed like a "no brainer" at this point so I bought the mower. The added intangible benefit was that lawns were easier to mow given the power supplied by the Briggs and Stratton engine. Intangible benefits are worth considering but are only useful when added to a concrete, highly quantifiable primary benefit. As a compelling reason to proceed, they generally won't stand on their own. Think of them as the "icing on the cake."

This obviously is an over simplified example. If you wanted to gain more accuracy and completeness in your analysis you'd factor in other expenses like gasoline and maintenance costs for the mower. Nevertheless, it is a simple example that illustrates how the payback period can be a powerful tool to convey attractiveness of the investment. As you rally for resources, you'll need some convincing rationale to support your requests. This is one of several techniques for adding weight to your argument.

Be reasonably thorough in your analysis but don't get stuck in the "analysis paralysis" trap. In other words, don't overdo it. The conclusions you draw from your analysis are only as good as the assumptions you make. Remember, these are estimates. Concentrate on the big number drivers and stick with whole numbers. It's also OK to round the larger ones.

For example, suppose your spreadsheet shows a benefit amount of $50,332.34. When you present this as justification in a later phase you may want to round it to $50,330 or even $50,000. Not only is this easier to grasp and remember, it also shows that you recognize that it is only an estimate. Your audience will know that the final result probably won't work out to the exact number shown on your PowerPoint slide but their take-away will be that it's a big and compelling number. That's what you want them to remember.

Another point worth mentioning is that the lawn business example illustrates an investment in an asset (the mower) to demonstrate the payback period. This approach is equally suitable for analysis of a project. After all, the project will have a cost associated with it and will presumably generate a quantifiable benefit.

Let's return to our EMR ISV testing and certification initiative and calculate the payback period. We know that our estimate of the project cost is $120,820 over the six-month duration of the project. What we don't know at this point is the primary benefit of this investment.

You go back to your sales manager and ask her if she could be a little more specific on what impact an EMR certified solution would have on your company's sales. She states that she knows of at least 100 potential customer opportunities for a sale of this product in the very first year. Although she and her sales team would love to capture all 100 opportunities, she is sales-savvy and realistic. She knows that competition from other companies is fierce and some sales would be lost to them. Furthermore, some customers will decide to "make do" with their existing EMR systems and would push off a purchase decision to a future year.

After discussing this with some senior members on her team and some historical sales analysis she thinks her team could capture at least 24% of these opportunities. These would be short-term sales, closed in the first year. She is confident in her estimate and states that it is a *conservative* one.

It is now easy to calculate an estimate of the number of sales in the first year that would be made possible by the certification testing project.

> 24% of 100 opportunities = 24 sales

> or

> About 2 sales per month.

Although the number of sales is a good start, you still don't know how beneficial these sales would be to your company. Sales Revenue and Profitability are two common and easily understood metrics. You then ask her what the Average Selling Price would be for each system. She pulls out her calculator and totals up the selling prices for the servers, network switches and storage array. She arrives at what she feels is a pretty good estimate of the Average Selling Price.

> Average selling price = $60,000

You can now calculate an estimate of the Sales Revenue per month.

> 2 sales x $60,000 per sale = $120,000 per month first year sales revenue

Sales Revenue only tells part of the story. To get a good picture of how beneficial these sales would really be to your company you must also know how profitable they are. If the profit on each sale is minuscule, there probably will be little to no benefit at all.

It would be nice to know how much profit is made on each sale. Gross Profit on sales is the difference between the Selling Price and its Product Cost. To figure this, a starting point can be Gross Profit Margin, also known as Gross Margin. This is a good metric because it is usually well known and easily understood in sales environments.

You go back to your sales manager and ask if she knows what the Average Gross Margin is on sales. She and her team are very familiar with this metric because they are compensated on it. She knows from experience that the average sale's Gross Margin is around 40%.

Since you now know the Revenue and the Gross Margin, you calculate the monthly Gross Profit for the first year.

> Gross Profit = Revenue x Gross Margin

> $120,000 Revenue per Month x 40% Gross Margin = $48,000 Gross Profit Per Month

Gross Profit is a rough indicator of profitability but it doesn't consider expenses other than Cost of Goods Sold or Taxes. However, it is a good bellwether of profit potential. Since we are dealing with broad estimates, Gross Profit will be good enough for our purposes.

We now have enough information to calculate the Payback Period for our project.

$$Payback\ Period = \frac{Cost\ of\ the\ Investment}{Periodic\ Cash\ Flow\ Generated\ by\ the\ Investment}$$

$$\frac{\$120{,}820\ Project\ Cost}{\$48{,}000\ Monthly\ Gross\ Profit} = Payback\ Period\ of\ 2.5\ months$$

Return on Investment

Another useful metric for determining how attractive an investment is Return on Investment or ROI. It is calculated as follows:

$$ROI = \frac{Net\ Profit\ from\ Investment\ Over\ the\ Period}{Investment\ x\ 100}$$

We first calculate the Gross Profit for the first year from the monthly Gross Profit:

$48,000 Gross Profit per Month x 12 months = $576,000 First Year Gross Profit

Now that we have the gross profit for the first year and the cost of the investment, we can plug them into the ROI formula:

$$\frac{\$576{,}000\ Gross\ Profit\ From\ Investment\ for\ 1\ Year}{\$120{,}820\ Project\ Cost\ x\ 100} = 477\%\ ROI$$

That is a whopping ROI! I should mention that a professional financial analyst would be more granular in his approach for calculating this. As mentioned, he probably would include more expenses in the cost figure which would increase total project cost. He would most likely use EBITA (Earnings Before Interest, Taxes and Amortization) instead of Gross Profit. EBITA paints a more accurate picture of earnings. Both of these adjustments would have the effect of lowering the effective ROI. However, a ROI of 477% is a very big return that leaves a lot of room for downward adjustment before the point is reached where the investment is deemed unattractive.

Remember, I said this book is about leadership and this analysis might seem like a lot to swallow. Have faith that we're not trying to become professional financial analysts. Our objective is to make some broad-brush but credible estimates to determine how compelling the pursuit of our goal would be. We need to first convince ourselves that it is worth it. If not, we should qualify out. Once we pass this gate, we can take our message to the stakeholders. We will be discussing that in a later stage.

The examples I have given are simple but limited. You will probably have other ways to measure success that apply to your unique project and industry. You may want to go a bit deeper but make sure you avoid the *analysis paralysis* quagmire. Be creative but always focus on credibility.

To review, our project looks very compelling. The investment pays for itself in a relatively short 2- ½ month period and has a significant ROI of 477% based on gross profit. Those are eye catching numbers. Armed with these metrics, you have a reasonable rationale to justify the pursuit of this goal.

Resources

The English Oxford Living Dictionary defines Resources as:

> *A stock or supply of money, materials, staff, and other assets that can be drawn on by a person or organization in order to function effectively.*

When I was in elementary school, I loved building things with my hands. At the time, I had little or no money so I had to scrounge for left over scraps of material in my parents' basement. Nevertheless, I was able to muster enough resources to build a variety of contraptions including several large kites, a couple of soap box derby karts and on one occasion a kayak. The kayak was my first foray into the world of water sports.

My father drove me to our local pond where I took my kayak on its maiden voyage. I ventured out several hundred feet from shore using a borrowed double paddle. As I glided over the water I turned and saw my father waving and giving me a big thumbs up. My voyage was a success so I turned around and paddled through the lily pads for a safe return to shore.

Back at home, the news of my kayak quickly spread. One of my friends was so envious that he offered to buy my kayak for $7. He was a year older and a bit taller than me but we both agreed he would probably still fit into the kayak. After some soul-searching and thoughtful deliberation, I decided to take the $7 and he became the new owner.

He couldn't contain his excitement and wanted to take the kayak to water immediately. We put the kayak on a wagon and moved it to our local frog pond that was about a ¼ mile from my house. The pond was only about three feet deep at its center and was teeming with bullfrogs and green algae. We slowly lowered the kayak through the algae and into the water. My friend then assumed his position in the cockpit.

He paddled out to the center of the pond but quickly found out that the kayak couldn't support his extra weight. The soft pinewood battens started to crack and dislodge and water poured in over the gunnels. A few seconds later, he was standing waste deep in the center of the pond. As he trudged back through the muck to the shore, he dragged the water laden kayak behind him. It continued to collapse and now looked like a folded-up bundle of sticks wrapped in water-logged fabric.

He seemed a bit upset at this point. Upon further examination he discovered that I had built the kayak from some old wooden moldings and a painted bed sheet for the fabric covering. While dripping wet and covered with sprigs of bright green algae, he demanded his money back. He complained that it was made from junk. He was older and bigger than me so I thought it would prudent to return his money, which I did.

I later thought that if I had access to better quality materials, this might not have happened. This was one of my earliest lessons in the importance of good resources.

Your end product or likelihood of goal achievement will rely heavily on the quality of resources you engage. The kayak example demonstrated the need for better material resources, but human resources are equally important. Always strive to get the very best resources possible, especially since your goal is a stretch. You want to be leading a varsity team with the best equipment, not the JVs with hand-me downs.

Let's return to our EMR ISV certification example. In the Feasibility activity you identified the resources needed to achieve the goal of a successful EMR ISV certification. This included identifying human resources by role and lab resources. That exercise made it possible to estimate costs which could be used to calculate return on investment in the Justification activity.

Human Resources

It is now time to identify specific resources that will fit the roles needed for your project. You need to associate names with the roles. You probably already had preliminary discussions with several of these professional individuals when you arrived at your level of effort estimate earlier in your planning. You will probably find that these same people love to talk about their roles and what they do for your organization. Your challenge will be to get enough face- or phone-time with them as they are usually very busy. Having lunch with them or buying coffee is a good venue for discussion. Face-to-face meetings are always the best format for discussions but you may not always have that luxury.

If they are located remotely and you can't travel to their location, you'd need to have a phone conversation. Try to avoid a back and forth email exchanges other than to set up a phone appointment. Email tends to be very impersonal and many people don't like to type out their thoughts on a computer screen. It can be down-right irritating to them. When you set up the phone or face-to-face appointments, be specific on what you would like to discuss and why. A sentence or two should be sufficient. They will appreciate your brevity and your respect for their time. Try to make the initial contact no more than fifteen or twenty minutes long.

You can think of yourself as a scout for a major professional sports team. You are looking for the best individual talent for each role as well as their ability to play well together with the rest of the team. When speaking with potential team players, make sure you don't come across as an interviewer. Instead, ask for their advice and feedback. Tell them what you are trying to accomplish and what it would mean for the success of your company.

Virtually all A-Player employees have a strong interest in contributing to their company's success. State why you sought them out in particular. Most people are flattered when someone values their input and is sincere in asking for their advice. Ask them about other projects they worked on and how their experiences might relate to your project. Given their role and specific expertise, what risks might arise over the course of your project? Do they have recommendations for how those risks can be mitigated? What is their assessment of your chances for achieving your goal? Have you overlooked anything? Who can they recommend to fill the other roles you have identified? Ask for introductions. Always be respectful and never patronizing.

As your dialog with each potential team member unfolds, you will be developing working relationships and garnering credibility. Their interest in participating in your project may percolate to the surface in the early stages of your conversations. After your initial meetings, you should strive for follow-on meetings for deeper dives into the details. You can invite multiple team members to a single meeting to get multiple perspectives. This also serves to kick off team dynamics with intra-team dialog. These appointments can be longer than the fifteen to twenty-minute initial contacts but no longer than forty-five minutes to an hour at most.

In these follow-on meetings you should show confidence and be succinct as you lay out the project's objective, why it is important to the company and what would be expected from each role. At some point, ask them directly if they would be interested in participating. You can do this collectively or individually. Most people want to be on a winning team, especially if they know they can be a major contributor to the team's success.

You will need to make a subjective judgement on how deep to go and how many meetings to have before filling out your team roster. Don't belabor the process but get enough feedback to make informed choices. Always make sure you come to each meeting prepared and make good use of the time you are given. Start each meeting promptly and finish on time. The best way to poison a team's interest is to waste their time. Don't do it!

At the end of this exercise, you should have a list of your top picks for each player by role. You should also have a secondary list of your alternate player picks by role. Mick Jagger of The Rolling Stones once sang "You can't always get what you want, you get what you need." Like Mick's lyric, that's where your secondary list of alternates could come in handy. You will also need a contingency list in case any of your primary players get sick, leave the company or get pulled off the project for other unexpected reasons.

Your list will have different roles and names but the format should look like one shown in Table 8 below.

Role	Primary	Alternate
Performance Engineer	John Phillips	Steve Wang
Lab Technician	Phil Caruso	Moira Kelly
Systems Engineer	Steve Wang	Sue Armstrong

Product Manager	Andrea Hicks	Tom Henderson
Leader	John Patton (that's you)	-

Table 8 - Team Members by Role

Upon further examination you notice that most of the technical team reports into a single engineering manager. The product manager is the only role that reports up through a different manager. This is not always the case in cross-functional teams. In many scenarios, human resources are sourced from multiple departments and reporting structures which adds complexity. Fortunately, our example is fairly straightforward and simple.

Now that we've identified our potential team, we need to focus on identifying which Lab Resources will give us the best probability of hitting our target of 5,000 transaction per second with the infrastructure we have chosen.

After several conversations with potential team members we find that there are three lab possibilities:

1. **Corporate Headquarters Lab**. A state-of-the art lab located 1,000 miles away at Corporate Headquarters. This lab has all imaginable combinations of the latest and fastest generations of equipment one might need for testing.

2. **Regional Lab**. A smaller lab in a regional office located 250 miles away. This lab doesn't have as wide a variety of equipment but does have the specific latest and fastest generation of servers, switches and storage array needed for our testing

3. **Local Lab**. A minimal lab that is housed in the same building as our potential test team. This lab has previous generation servers which aren't quite as fast as the latest generation servers the other labs have. This lab also has switches and a storage array which are identical to these equipment types found in the other two labs.

All three labs have the requisite 225 square feet of space needed to house the equipment and perform the testing.

Your first inclination is to pick The Regional Lab because it has the latest generation equipment and it is not as far away as the Corporate Headquarters Lab. The downside is that your team would still need to travel 250 miles to the site to set up the equipment and perform the testing. This would incur extra travel and lodging costs and this might inhibit the team's willingness to participate or their general availability. For some team members this would mean multiple weeks away from their home and day-to-day work location. Could you sell this idea? It would definitely be a harder sell than keeping the team local.

Know When to Push and When to Concede

After more discussion with your performance engineer you find that slightly slower servers would not have a material impact on this test. He explains that the critical performance component will be the storage array, not the servers. Since the Local Lab has the latest generation storage array you can make an informed decision to proceed with that venue.

This is an example of when it is wise to make a concession on resources. Although the servers are slightly slower than those found in the other two labs, it is not worth insisting that the testing be done in either of those labs. This would only increase the cost of the project and possibly put the human resource availability in jeopardy.

Although this example demonstrates a clear-cut choice, not all resource decisions are this easy. You will need to gather as much information as you can to make the best-informed decisions. Know when to push and when to concede. Can you make a concession without jeopardizing the likelihood of reaching your goal? Your flexibility will be appreciated and will add weight to your credibility.

Review

Table 9 below summarizes what we've accomplished so far in the Four Phases of our Planning Activity.

	Planning Phase
Idea	1. Identified a business challenge – Need to increase revenues and margins 2. Picked a potential solution from a list of choices – Expand into new untapped markets
Feasibility	1. Identified a way to expand into a new market – Enable new sales by testing and certifying an EMR infrastructure solution for the Healthcare market 2. Identifled target for success – 5,000 transactions per second using six servers, two switches and a single storage array 3. Determined likelihood of success – Consulted performance expert who determined goal is a stretch but achievable 4. Identified generic resources needed – Human resources by role and Lab & Equipment 5. Estimated project costs – Human resources and lab & equipment
Justification	1. Determined market size – Calculated sales and gross profit potential 2. Determined if project is worth the investment – Calculated Payback Period and Return on Investment
Resources	1. Identified the team – Identified primary and alternate team players by name 2. Identified the venue – selected the least cost lab venue without jeopardizing goal achievement

Table 9 - Planning Activity Summary

The key is not the will to win...everybody has that. It is the will to prepare to win that is important.

-Bobby Knight

Chapter 3: Selling the Stakeholders

Stakeholders

The noun *stakeholder* can have many meanings, depending on the context in which it is used. The meaning that closely fits our use of this term is defined by yourdictionary.com as follows:

> *The definition of a stakeholder is a person who has an interest in or investment in something and who is impacted by and cares about how it turns out.*

To illustrate this concept, consider the following fictitious example.

Marvin just turned 52 years old and last month he fell victim to a moderate heart attack. Fortunately, he survived but his doctor advised him that the blood flow to his heart was not healthy and he should get expert advice from a heart specialist. He recommended Dr. Patel who had many years of experience treating heart patients and had earned an impeccable reputation as a skilled surgeon.

After some soul-searching and discussion with his wife Eunice, Marv decided to follow his doctor's recommendation and seek out Dr. Patel. After extensive testing and clinical analysis, Dr. Patel broke the news to Marv and Eunice that, unless he had heart bypass surgery he may not survive another heart attack. The doctor went on to explain that although heart bypass surgery is a common operation, it is not without risk.

Marv and Eunice decided to notify their son Stuart who was away at college studying the migratory patterns of Arctic terns. In a casual conversation, Stuart mentioned the news of his dad's heart condition to Leon, his dormitory roommate. Leon had a scholarship for horseshoe distance throwing but admitted he had difficulty hitting the stake. He hadn't known Stuart for very long and stated the news did not sound good.

With Eunice and Stuart's encouragement, Marv decided to proceed with the operation. Dr. Patel performed the procedure with great skill and without incident and Marv made a full recovery. Everyone's wishes had come true and the story had a happy ending.

In this whimsical and somewhat irreverent story, we can now identify the following:

1. Who the stakeholders are and
2. What their interests are in a successful outcome

Stakeholder Identification

Is Marv a stakeholder? Obviously! He had an overwhelming interest in the outcome of the operation. He enjoyed life and wanted to keep it that way. He was not ready to visit the Pearly Gates.

Is Eunice a stakeholder? Absolutely! She loved her husband and always wanted the best for him. If she were to lose him, she would be heart-broken for a very long time.

Is Stuart a stakeholder? Definitely! He loves his Dad and would be crushed if Marv didn't make it. Marv was always his best pal and was the one who got him interested in Arctic terns.

Is Leon a stakeholder? Probably not. Although he never wished any harm would come to Stuart's dad, he didn't know Stuart very well and was somewhat detached from the situation. Although he would probably feel badly for a few days after news of a failed operation, he otherwise would be unaffected.

Is Dr. Patel a stakeholder? Affirmative! He was the doctor performing the operation and had a strong interest in a successful surgery. He carried an enormous responsibility knowing that the operation had inherent risk and Marv's family was counting on him to deliver.

Was Marv's referring doctor a stakeholder? We could make a case either way. If we consider him a stakeholder, he probably would have a minor interest in the outcome when compared to the other stakeholders. He made a good recommendation in Dr. Patel and most of the responsibility for a successful operation was borne by the heart surgeon. For this case, we won't consider him as a stakeholder.

Stakeholder Interests

Now that we have identified the stakeholders, we can proceed to identify their vested interests in a successful operation outcome. The strongest and most overriding interest shared by all stakeholders is their concern for Marv's life and well-being.

Other stakeholder interests may not be as strong or as obvious. Let's examine each in more detail.

Marv was concerned that he was the sole breadwinner of his family. If his operation ended badly, his family would no longer have a means of financial support. That worried him.

Eunice shared Marv's concern and pondered the prospect of having to get a full-time job to support herself and pay for Stuart's studies. Like Marv, she was in her early fifties and the thought of needing to work was depressing. This was a difficult issue for her to cope with and the thought of it kept her up a night.

Stuart thought that his studies might be jeopardized if the operation was not successful. He loathed the possibility of having to drop out of college due to lack of tuition funding. He also thought that his knowledge of Artic terns might be difficult to sell in the job market. The uncertainty bothered him greatly.

As mentioned, Dr. Patel had an impeccable record of successfully heart operations. He was in high demand because of his stellar reputation. If the operation was not successful, it might blemish his standing in the medical community and possibly put a damper on future referrals. Even worse, he might become the target of a malpractice lawsuit. Although he took steps to protect himself through signed legal documents, the current litigious climate worried him.

We can now summarize our findings in Table 10 below:

Player	Stakeholder	Interest in Successful Outcome
Marv	Yes	• Continue living a natural life • Continue providing family with financial stability
Eunice	Yes	• Preserve husband's life and well-being • No need to find a job and work full-time
Stuart	Yes	• Preserve father's life and well-being • No need to drop out of college • No need to search for a job with arcane skillset
Leon	No	n/a
Dr. Patel	Yes	• Preserve patient's life and well-being • Keep stellar reputation intact • Continue referrals at current fast clip • Eliminate threat of malpractice lawsuit
Referring Doctor	No	n/a

Table 10 - Stakeholder Interest Summary – Successful Operation

The exercise that we just completed demonstrates the process by which we can identify a project's stakeholders and their particular motivations or interests in achieving the goal. The overriding interest shared by all was saving Marv's life and well-being. There were also other interests that were specific to each stakeholder.

In this case, the decision to proceed with the Marv's operation was a "no brainer" and no persuasion was necessary to get buy-in from the stakeholders. This usually is *not* the case in the business world. Selling is required.

Remember, you will be leading a team of individuals who are not under your direct control. There is always a financial cost associated with this. You probably will also be asking for additional resources that require funding. You will need to be persuasive in convincing the key stakeholders why your goal is important, particularly to them. Your reasoning must be compelling. The stakeholders will be making decisions based on whether the perceived benefits outweigh the costs. For this reason, you should prepare for this by going through this process by identifying who the key stakeholders are and why they should give you the "green light" to proceed.

Selling the Stakeholders involves four distinct activities that are outlined in Figure 3 below.

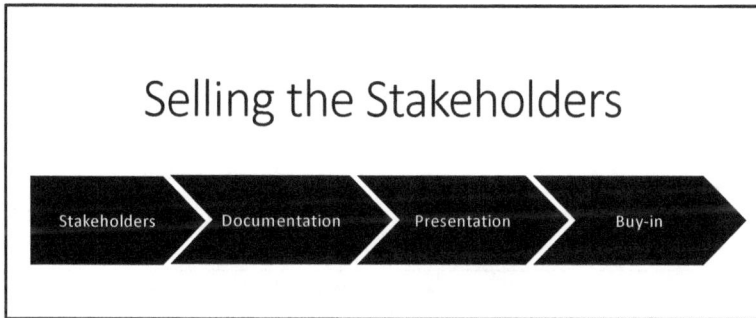

Selling the Stakeholders

Stakeholders → Documentation → Presentation → Buy-in

Figure 3 - Selling the Stakeholders Phase

We have already seen how we can identify the stakeholders and their interests in Marv's successful operation. We will be discussing the Documentation, Presentation and Buy-in activities later on in this chapter. Before we continue, however, let's continue applying our stakeholder identification techniques to the EMR certification example discussed in the previous chapter. Table 11 is probably a reasonable summary.

Player	Stakeholder	Interest in Successful Outcome
Senior Sales Executive	Yes	• Increase overall sales and margins • Make more sales commission dollars • Increase positive recognition by senior management • Better chance of promotion • Increased job security
Your Manager	Yes	• Expand into Heathcare market segment • Capture sales otherwise conceded to the competition • Increase positive recognition by management • Increase chance of future salary increases • Better chance of promotion
Performance Engineer	Yes	• Opportunity to demonstrate specialized skills • Prove relevancy to the organization • Increase job security • Increase chance of future salary increases • Increase recognition of being expert in the field
Lab Technician	Yes	• Opportunity to learn from more senior staff members • Add additional skills and experience to resume • Better chance of promotion
Systems Engineer	Yes	• Opportunity to gain addional hands on experience • Add addional skills and experience to resume • Increase positive recognition by management • Better chance of promotion
Product Manager	Yes	• Increase sales of products under management • Increase positive recognition by management • Better chance of promotion
Engineering Manager	Yes	• Increase positive recognition by management • Better chance of future salary increases • Better chance of promotion
Sales Force	Yes	• More products that can be sold • Better chance of achieving sales quotas • Make more sales commission dollars • Increased job security
EMR ISV Partner Alliance Manager	Yes	• Offer customers an additional choice of infrastructure on which to run their EMR software • More incremental sales revenue

Table 11 - Stakeholder Interest Summary - EMR Certification Testing

Documentation

Briefing Document

After graduating from college, Stuart was excited to land his first job as a Birdwatching Tour Guide at a local wildlife sanctuary. His place of work was about twenty miles from his house and he needed reliable transportation to it. Although his moped served him well in college, he knew it was time to move on to a good reliable car.

His mother, Eunice, also welcomed Stuart's decision to retire his moped. Although she admired the Arctic tern decal on the tank, she had always worried that it might lead him into joining an outlaw motorcycle gang.

After searching the World Wide Web to narrow down his choices, Stuart visited a few dealers and scrutinized each vehicle close up. Although he was extremely nervous, he took each car out for a spin around the block. After a close call with a school bus, he breathed a sigh of relief that he was able to return safely.

Stuart quickly discovered that all of the automobiles came with a variety of engine and trim options. The EPA gas mileage ratings were yet another consideration. After listening to competing sales pitches from several pompous salesmen, Stuart's head was spinning trying to remember all of the particular selling points and advantages of each vehicle.

Most of the salesmen were impatient for a quick sale and didn't bother to invest any more time in Stuart. However, one astute salesman recognized that Stuart merely wanted to give his decision a little more thought. Perhaps he also wanted to solicit some advice from his family and friends. The salesman gave Stuart a glossy multipage brochure that he could take home with him. In addition to the gorgeous photographs of the automobile, all the specifications, selling points and options were included.

Stuart wasn't ready to make a hasty decision on a big purchase like an automobile. He put the brochure on his breakfast bar. Every morning he picked it up and browsed through the beautiful photographs and selling points. He also showed it to his dad, Marv, who wasn't able to visit the showrooms with Stuart that day. He happened to be out riding his pet Ostridge that weekend. Marv studied the brochure and was thoroughly impressed with what he saw. He then gave Stuart a big thumbs up.

A week later Stuart made the decision to purchase the car. He returned to the dealership, bought the car and thereafter was always prompt for work and ready to start his Birdwatching Tours on-time.

This example illustrates the important role that documentation plays in the selling process. This is frequently overlooked. The automobile brochure continued to move Stuart's buying decision in a positive direction long after he left the dealership. Furthermore, the brochure accurately conveyed the attractiveness of the automobile to Marv who wasn't present for the sales pitch. Since there were a myriad of factors to consider, Stuart probably couldn't communicate all them to his dad in a convincing and rational way. Using information gleaned from the brochure, Marv was able to make an informed recommendation based on a combination of facts and esthetic appeal. In short, the brochure sold Marv as well.

The importance of clear and concise documentation that describes what you are trying to achieve and why cannot be over stated. You are in the process of marshalling a team and other resources that are not under your direct control. You will need to convey a compelling case to the stakeholders who have the authority to grant you the resources. Without supporting documentation, your case will be far more difficult to make. Each stakeholder's decision whether to provide resources or not is usually not done on the spot as we found with Stuart's car decision.

Once you present your case in a formal presentation or conference call, there is usually a deliberation phase that follows. Rarely will stakeholders make an immediate decision. They typically need time to internalize what they've heard. They will probably want to discuss it with their cohorts and superiors to get their opinions. This is especially true if you are requesting a significant amount of funding or need the participation of a large cross-functional team. The decision makers will most likely weigh the perceived benefits of your goal versus other projects that are competing for the resources. After all, resources within an organization are never infinite and there are always tradeoffs to consider.

What are the chances these decision makers will remember all of selling points you made to them? Not likely! They are "holding the purse strings" and are the "gate keepers" of the resources. Because of this, they are usually inundated with many other competing requests that are vying for the same resources. This can be confusing and a bit mind boggling for them.

There may also be other influencers involved in the decision, like Marv, whom you may never have the opportunity to meet. For them, your documentation will be the selling vehicle. Doesn't it make sense to provide a "brochure" or "cheat sheet" that everyone can refer to when deliberating their decision?

As mentioned earlier, documentation is frequently overlooked because it takes considerable time and discipline to accurately commit the relevant facts and selling points to paper. Be sure to take the extra time and discipline to document your case. Rest assured it *will* pay off. Always keep those selling points front and center!

Let's take a closer look at what your supporting document might look like. The term *brochure* usually describes a glossy, multi-color pamphlet that is used to sell a product or service. It doesn't really fit our purpose because we are not selling a product or service. We are pursuing a goal and need resources to achieve it.

We also used the term *cheat sheet*. This term might be appropriate as informal jargon to describe the intended purpose of your document. However, it can have a dark connotation that can be misconstrued. Are you asking the stakeholders to cheat? Of course not, but there are better terms for naming your document.

You don't need to be elaborate. *Planning Document, Planning Brief* or *Briefing Document* are simple, straightforward terms that are easy to understand. You can use one of these terms or a similar one when referring to your document.

You may be wondering what you should include in your Planning Brief. Although this can vary depending on the nature of your goal and required resources, the following is a general outline that can apply to many situations:

- Cover Page
- Table of Contents
- Executive Summary
- Background
- Objective
- Benefits
- Resources
- Timeframe
- Appendix

Let's take a look at each one of these sections in more detail.

Cover Page

A cover page is the simplest section to write. You should include the title of your goal or project, your name and the current date on this page. You may also want to include a revision number as you may modify this document several times as you move through the process. In preliminary meetings you may get feedback that you had inadvertently overlooked something important. Other points may need further clarification.

Use a large and bold font to make the title stand out. Your name and the date should be shown with less emphasis. The cover will be the very first optic that your reader's eyeballs will be drawn to. Remember the old saying "you never get a second chance to make a first impression." Make sure your cover is clear, well laid out and visually pleasing.

The judicious use of color and graphics such as simple lines can enhance the esthetic appeal of your cover. If appropriate, you may want to include your company logo. Be aware that occasionally corporate attorneys will object to this. However, it is usually permissible to include a logo if the document is intended solely for internal consumption and marked as such.

If you intend to distribute your document outside your company such as to a partner company or a customer, you should first consider getting advice from your marketing or legal department. You may find that you will need to include some legal mumbo-jumbo disclaimer text on the reverse side of the cover. If you are not sure about this, check with your appropriate authorities.

You may find templates that already exist that will give your cover a professional look. Just try not to make it look like it was produced with a "cookie cutter." It always helps to establish your own brand through the creative use of fonts, color and simple graphics.

Table of Contents

A table of contents can be easily generated if you format your document using headings. For example, the section you are reading right now has a heading above it called "Table of Contents." MS Word can automatically generate a Table of Contents for you using the Headings you included in your document. This includes page numbers and the text of each heading with appropriate indentations, depending on the heading levels you used. You also have numerous choices of fonts and layouts.

If you are not sure how to include this, do a Web search on it or explore your word processor's help facility. You should find that it is easy to include a table of contents both for the initial iteration and for any updates you later make to the body of the document.

For short documents of just a few pages, a table of contents is probably overkill and you may not want to include one. However, for documents that are longer than six or seven pages, A table of contents can provide your readers with a handy reference that will quickly point them to the material they are most interested in. Many readers won't take the time to read your entire document. A properly formatted table of contents can also give your document a polished and professional look that can enhance their first impression.

Executive Summary

The executive summary is a one or two paragraph summary of your document. It is probably the most important section of your document because it is the most frequently read. As mentioned earlier, many of your readers won't take the time to read your entire document. They will probably skip to the executive summary and scan the rest. For these impatient and time-challenged readers you need to make sure your summary is clear, concise and delivers a targeted and convincing message.

You need to convey 1) What your goal is 2) Why is it beneficial to both the company and the individual stakeholders and 3) A high level description of what you need to achieve it. Make sure you understand your audience's interests and pay particular attention to #2 above. In addition to the overall company's interests, you should also address what's in it for them? Go back to the stakeholder interest summary that you developed in the previous section. Note that most of their interests are of a personal nature. You would never want to make a direct reference to them like "My goal will get you a promotion." That would be good way to get your document placed in the "circular file" next to their desk.

Instead, you can make indirect references to their interests and rely on them to make the connection. For example, you may use the phrase *high visibility* when you are describing your goal. For those that are interested in a possible promotion, the fact that your goal will be noticed at high levels in the organization is key to their personal interests. Who wouldn't want to be associated with a successful high visibility project? They can later say "I was part of that."

Salespeople are interested in making money. For them, you might use phrases such as *increase sales* and *expand product portfolio*. It will be easy for them to make the connection to their personal interests regarding more commission dollars.

You will need to carefully sort out the personal interests and identify possible linkages to overall company benefits. It will take some careful thought. When you are done composing your summary, you will need to take a step back and examine whether you successfully addressed stakeholders' interests. You may not be able to address all of them in a short summary. Look for the "low hanging fruit" and address that first. Get your most important points across but avoid being too verbose. Remember, this is a summary and not a treatise on your life's ambitions. One or two paragraphs should be sufficient.

The executive summary can be written at a couple of different points during the documentation process. It can be written up-front before the rest of the document is completed. Alternatively, it can be written at the very end of the process. It is a matter of personal preference. Some authors prefer to write the summary last as it is easier to ensure that all critical points in the document are included. Although we focused on the #2 topic above that describes "Why it is beneficial", make sure you cover all three topics listed at the beginning of this section in your executive summary.

Background

The background section is the "set up" for the Planning Brief. It answers the question "How did we get here?" What were the events that created a need to pursue this goal? What sparked the pursuit? In the EMR Certification example, some of the background was a need to boost sales revenues and margins, expand into a critical growth market and stop conceding sales to the competition due to a lack of a tested and certified solution.

You can go into more detail in this section but always stay focused on the compelling reasons for pursuing the goal. You are telling a story that should support your case. Sell the story but be objective and honest and above all, avoid hyperbole. You are in the process of building credibility. Be persuasive but don't be a "Chicken Little" with "The Sky is Falling" alarm.

Objective

The objective is what you hope to achieve if you are given the resources. It's the goal that you have in mind. This section should be brief and to the point. You should be able to describe this in a single paragraph in just a few sentences.

Benefits

The benefits section is one that you should pay particular attention to. This is the "make-or-break" section that is the justification for pursuing your goal. Why should the decision makers and influencers grant you the resources you are asking for? You will answer that question in this section.

You performed your due diligence in the Qualification and Quantification activities of the Planning phase. By now, you should have enough material to draw upon to present a convincing case. This may include metrics such as the short payback period, the sizeable return on investment, increased sales revenue, fat gross margins or other key performance indicators you think are important.

Cherry pick the most salient points and put them up front in your narrative. Consider including graphs and diagrams to support your assertions. Remember the old idiom "A picture is worth a thousand words." Just make sure your diagrams are intelligible and relevant. A complicated or confusing graph will dilute the impact of your story. Exclude any points that don't significantly add weight to your argument. A good rule of thumb is adherence to the KISS principle "Keep It Simple, Stupid."

Resources

The resources section is usually a "drop in" of the analysis you did earlier in the Resources phase of the Planning activity. Include a table that lists the required human resources by role with individual names included. Only include your first choices and omit the alternates. Why make it easy for decision makers to immediately skip to your second choices? You can always revisit this later if conflicts arise.

Other first choice resources should be listed in the same way. Although not necessary, you may want to consider adding a brief reason why you chose a particular resource. These reasons will be specific to your resource requests but could include such factors as close proximity, ease of access, most efficient, etc.

Costs should not be included in this section. Costs have a negative connotation and generally should be avoided. Costs should only be discussed in the context of the benefits they offer. The benefits section is a much better place to discuss them. That way, the benefits will create an opposing offset that will have a dampening effect on any perceived "sticker shock."

Timeframe

The timeframe section should display a high-level estimate of the total project duration with the associated resource requirements. The best way to describe this is with a timeline graph that consists of a horizontal line divided with equal date marks. A simple horizontal time divided by weeks or months is usually adequate. An example is shown in Figure 4 below.

Project Timeline

Resources

Product Manager
Lab Tech
Lab Tech
Performance Engineer
Systems Engineer
Lab

Apr   May   Jun   Jul   Aug   Sep

Activities

Product Evaluation
Testing and Tuning
Lab Setup
Partner Evaluation
Lab Breakdown

Certification Goal Achieved

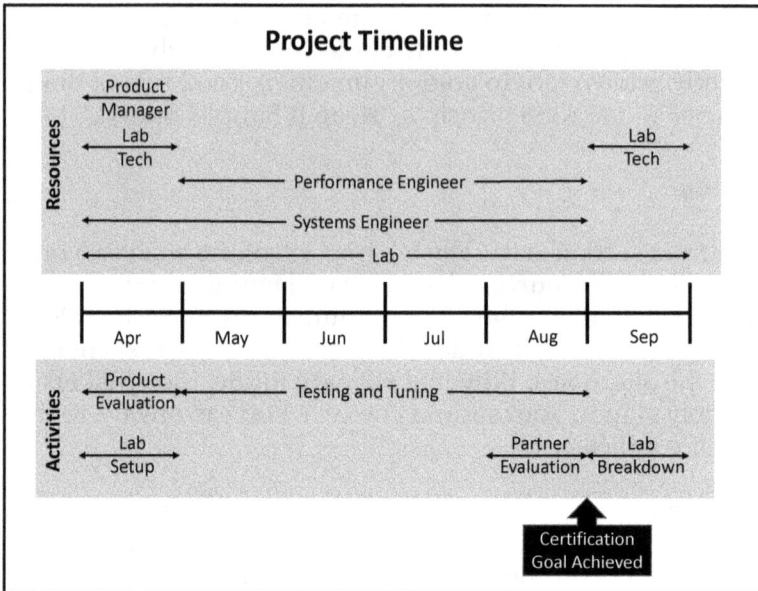

Figure 4 - Sample Timeline

Resources are added to the timeline with their associated start and end dates. Major projected milestone events are then overlaid on the timeline. This isn't intended to be a detailed project plan but merely a high-level estimate of when resources are required and for how long. Again, simplicity is the rule.

Appendix

You may or may not want to include an appendix. The appendix is where you put supporting information that may be too detailed for inclusion in the main body of your Planning Brief. You may have a graph that takes a considerable amount of effort to comprehend but nevertheless adds weight to your case. The appendix is a good place to put this.

You may also have information that gives additional context regarding your plan but is too verbose for the main body of text.

This should go in the appendix. Think of the appendix as the "For further reading" section of your Planning Brief.

Presentation

You've done your homework. Your goal is centered in your crosshairs and you have plenty of compelling reasons for why you should pursue it. You have a well-researched list of the resources that you will need to achieve it. You've documented the major points in your Planning Brief. It is now time to present your case to the decision makers and influences who will ultimately grant you the resources.

Presentations can take many forms, depending on a variety of factors. These can include where the individual audience members are physically located, when they are available to participate, how much time they are willing to devote to the meeting, their size in number, the nature of the meeting place and how formal or informal the presentation should be. Another consideration is the skill level required to deliver an effective presentation.

Some of the common methods and media for delivering presentations are listed in Table 12 below.

Delivery Medium	Typical Venue	Proximity to Audience	Maximum Audience Size	Relative Formality	Relative Skill Needed for Delivery
PowerPoint Slides Local	Conference Room or Auditorium	Face-to-face	Medium	Formal	Low
Whiteboard	Conference Room	Face-to-face	Small	Semi-formal	Medium
Paper Easel	Conference Room	Face-to-face	Small	Semi-formal	Medium
Conversation	Office or Conference Room	Face-to-face	Small	Informal	High
Conference Call	Phone System	Remote	Large	Formal	Medium
Electronic Whiteboard	Internet + Software	Remote	Large	Semi-formal	High
PowerPoint Slides Over Internet	Internet + Software	Remote	Large	Formal	Medium

Table 12 - Presentation Delivery Methods

Let's examine each of these delivery mediums in a little more detail.

PowerPoint Slides Local

A PowerPoint presentation delivered locally is usually done in a conference room for small audiences. It is equally effective in an auditorium for large audiences. It lends itself to these venues because your presentation can be electronically projected from a laptop to a screen of any size.

It is arguably the easiest type of presentation to give because it can be scripted in advance. You also have a set of speakers notes right on the screen at times. The audience can follow along as you present your bullet points, diagrams and charts.

The downslide of PowerPoint presentations is that they tend to limit the presenter to what is shown on the screen. Some

66

audiences object to this format because of its scripted nature and perceived one-way communication. However, a skillful presenter can overcome these objections by asking questions of the audience and expanding on the points presented on the slides. Audience participation is always a good way to keep them engaged.

A major benefit of a PowerPoint presentation is the added flexibility of selecting and embedding key slides in your Briefing Document. This can give your document a more professional look that can generate more reader interest than a text-only document. An effective documentation technique is to develop your PowerPoint presentation prior to your Briefing Document. You can then wrap descriptive text around the key slide exhibits in your document. Just make sure you don't short change your message with too many slides and not enough descriptive text.

Whiteboard

A whiteboard presentation is a great vehicle for encouraging audience participation. Using dry erase markers, you outline your major points and graphics on a whiteboard. If a member of your audience has a question or needs clarification regarding a complex issue, you can hand her a marker and ask her to elaborate on the whiteboard. This gives your session an increased level of interactivity that can have the effect of drawing your audience into your train of thought.

Another benefit of the whiteboard presentation is that you can easily tailor the presentation on the fly to your audience. Unlike a PowerPoint presentation that has a canned and serial nature to it, you can easily jump directly to the areas of greatest interest for your particular audience.

A whiteboard presentation usually takes more skill to deliver than a PowerPoint presentation because you don't have detailed notes constantly in front of you. It takes some practice. However, it is worth investing the time in mastering it because most small audiences prefer this to a boring and scripted PowerPoint presentation.

Paper Easel

A paper easel or flip chart is almost identical to a whiteboard medium. The skill level required is roughly equivalent. The basic difference is that you can't erase what you have written on the paper. Since you will be flipping the paper sheets as you proceed through the presentation, points you made earlier in the presentation could be obscured. With a large whiteboard you can work from one side to the other with all points visible at all times. You can alleviate this potential drawback with a paper easel by ripping each sheet off as you complete it and taping it to the wall.

Unlike an erasable whiteboard, you are creating a permanent record on paper. This could be a potential security issue if you are discussing sensitive topics. In these cases, make sure you take the paper with you when you leave or hand it to a responsible audience member who may want to refer to it at a later time.

Conversation

A presentation delivered through conversation requires the highest level of skill. In these cases, you may be sitting across the desk from a senior executive who doesn't have the time or inclination to listen to a formal presentation. You will have a limited amount of time to make your case. An organized and focused delivery is essential. You will be riding bareback and won't have the luxury of presentation aides to rely on.

Become familiar with the concept of "the elevator pitch." You should be able to deliver your key points to a theoretical person sharing an elevator ride in the short amount of time it takes for the elevator to reach its destination floor. Practice it. You will use it many times.

Although these are the most difficult presentations to deliver effectively, they are also the most valuable. Many times, your audience will be senior level executives who will have the most influence in granting you the resources you are requesting.

Conference Call

Conference calls are useful for delivering presentations to audiences that are geographically disbursed. You will need a phone system that will allow many people to share a single line. A good way to set this up is via common calendaring systems such as MS Outlook. You can embed the dial-in number and access code in the calendar initiation you send. Some smart phones will dial the conference number and access code with one or two touches of the screen. This makes it convenient for audience members who are travelling.

When the start time has arrived, take a rollcall of everyone who is expected to be on the call. Many times, people will arrive a minute or two late due to previous meetings running late. For these participants, it is common courtesy to allow a few minutes extra time for them to join. However, don't allow it to extend much longer than this.

Make sure you communicate with the rest the team that are already on the line. Once everyone has joined, start the call immediately. Don't waste your audience's time with small talk. There is nothing more irritating than taking valuable time out of your day to hear someone railing on about the weather in their area. Keep the call on track but always be polite and courteous. Remember, your participants are giving up a part of their day to listen to you. Be sure to end your call on-time or slightly before. You audience will appreciate your respect for their time.

Conference calls don't require much more skill than that required for a standard PowerPoint presentation. You can have whatever notes you require in front of you. The only extra burden is working out the technical details involved in setting up the call. It is an effective and relatively low-cost method for reaching small to very large audiences in remote locations.

Electronic Whiteboard

A variation on a whiteboard presentation is an electronic whiteboard presentation. A computer is used with special software that mimics a whiteboard but can be displayed to an audience also running the software on computers connected to the Internet.

Voice-Over-IP (VOIP) usually accompanies this type of presentation and is included in the software. VOIP removes the need for a conventional phone system so all communication, both visual and verbal, can be done over a single Internet connection.

Not only does this presentation method require whiteboarding skills, you will also need to master the particular features of the software. If you decide to go this route, you will need to practice it to become proficient. Like a conference call, this technique can be used to reach a wide audience across many remote locates.

PowerPoint Slides Over Internet

Similar to the electronic whiteboard, a PowerPoint presentation can be delivered over the Internet. The software you will need is usually the same. Again, you will need to master the operation of the software so some practice may be necessary. Beyond that, it is no more difficult than giving a standard PowerPoint presentation. It is another method for reaching a large remote audience.

A variation of this is using a combination of a conference call and a PowerPoint deck. Using this method, you send the PowerPoint deck to the participants in advance. You then use the telephone conference call to deliver your voice while they follow along using their individual copies of the PowerPoint presentation.

Presentation Tips and Techniques

Most people experience some anxiety before giving a presentation. This is normal and even experienced presenters can feel an elevated heartbeat. Just remember that you've done your homework and you are the expert of the material you will be presenting. You will find that your nervousness will dissipate in the first 30 seconds of the presentation.

Above all you will need to project confidence. If you make a mistake in your presentation, state the correction with confidence and move on. It happens to the best of us. Focus your thoughts on the material and not on what you think the audience might be thinking.

You will need to decide how and when you want to handle questions from your audience. If the answer to a question is a simple one, you'll probably want to answer it right away and then move on. If the answer is more involved, you may want to save it for the end of the presentation. Encourage participation to keep your audience engaged but don't get pulled off topic. Going down a rathole is a sure way to derail an otherwise effective presentation. You'll need to be tactful in filtering out irrelevant dialog.

At times you will get legitimate questions that you hadn't anticipated and can't answer. Don't let this throw you off. Confidently take a note and state that you will get an answer. Be sure to follow up with the answer with the person that asked the question. You may also want to include the other members of the audience in your follow-up. This is a good way to keep your topic on their minds. You can't be expected to know everything and reasonable people understand that. This is a golden opportunity to gain additional credibility with a timely follow-up.

One of the most challenging aspects of presenting is handling detractors or hecklers. These are people who have already decided they don't want to support you. They typically ask questions that are purposely designed to derail or embarrass you. You will need to make a judgement on whether the question is legitimate or is a heckler question. For hecklers, "don't get mad, get even." I don't recommend that you turn over tables and throw things. If you show anger or animosity toward the heckler, they have accomplished their mission. A better way to handle a heckler's question is to ask them why the question is important to them. They may not have a good answer and it can serve to quiet them.

Humor is also good tension-breaker if used properly. Never make fun of the heckler but a friendly joke or two about your material can go a long way in diffusing an otherwise contentious situation. Other supportive audience members may come to your aid and express their distaste for the heckling. Use your best judgement, be respectful and use tact in handling these annoying cases.

When writing on a whiteboard or easel, avoid the common mistake of standing in front of it with your back to the audience. Have you ever heard the expression "You make a better door than a window?" Don't obscure the board with your back. Your audience wants to see what you are writing. Don't make them wait as this gives them an opportunity to "tune out." Instead, stand to the side as you mark on the board so they can see your presentation as it unfolds. It will take some practice do this is effectively. This is a technique that doesn't feel normal to many first-time users.

Have you ever stopped to think about the effect different colors have in your presentations? If you are developing a PowerPoint presentation you will probably use multiple colors to make it visually appealing. Colors can have a deeper meaning that you may not have considered. The color green for example, usually represents *go* or *good*. The color red usually signifies *stop, bad or alarm*. Yellow is somewhere in between although it doesn't show up very well on a PowerPoint slide. Think "traffic light" when you are developing your presentation. Use green to show a positive trend line or an improvement in a displayed metric. Similarly, red should be used to illustrate a negative or something you are striving to correct.

Black and blue colors are neutral colors. If you are using a dry erase whiteboard and only have one felt-tip marker to choose from, reach for a black one or a blue one. A whiteboard covered in red ink can possibly have a negative subliminal effect on your audience. When whiteboarding a topic, you might consider using multiple colors if you have the available markers. If you don't feel comfortable switching back and forth, stick with a single black or blue marker. Using colors in this way is a minor point. However, it worth considering if you want to add polish to your presentation.

Buy-In

The term *buy-in* has many meanings depending on the context in which it is used. This book is about employee or stakeholder buy-in. A good summary of this concept was expressed in a 2016 article written by Rick Conlow that appeared on Linkedin.com:

> *Buy-in is not a cute phrase or consultant speak. It's like a cause or movement, that transcends individual needs and issues. The employees become more than motivated. Their buy-in formulates into an inspired mental bond that synergizes the working relationship between people on the team. This leads to sustainable excellent performance, superior to those teams without it.*

Employee buy-in involves salesmanship. You need to assert a positive influence on others to get their buy-in. Before I go any further I'd like to explain what I mean by *salesmanship* as this term can have a negative connotation for many people. Who hasn't experienced the hard sell tactics of an overly aggressive car or insurance salesman? There are plenty of bad salesmen out there and we should avoid them. However, I believe that the sales profession as a whole is honorable and valuable even though it is sullied by the abusive practices of a small minority of bad actors.

I had a philosophical discussion on this topic a few years ago with a colleague of mine. Being a full-time salesman, he believed that his role had few redeeming virtues other than providing a lucrative income for him. I took issue with his viewpoint because he never came across as the high-pressure, hard-sell stereotype. I worked with him for several years and believed he always exhibited integrity and respect for his customers.

I explained to him that a good salesman is a valuable asset to customers who need advice. They have challenges they need to overcome. A good salesman will have a dialog with prospective customers and carefully listen to their needs. He will ask pertinent questions. Once a need is identified, he will honestly and objectively determine whether he can fulfill it with a product or service that he can offer. If he knows he can't help, he will qualify out and not waste the customer's time.

If he determines that he has a solution that will satisfy the customer's need he will propose it. By doing this, he is *helping* the customer and is acting as a trusted advisor. His self-interest is not of primary importance. His primary motivation is a mutual benefit, also called a *win-win* situation. The customer has a need and the salesman can fulfill it. Assuming he delivers on his promise at a reasonable price, the salesman gains the trust and respect he deserves. He will probably be welcomed back long after the sale is made.

Have you ever heard the expression "He is such a good salesman he could sell air conditioners to Eskimos?" Do you really think this person is a good salesman? I disagree with this misleading and worn out expression. He didn't fulfill any need and didn't act with integrity. He acted solely in self-interest. He is *not* a good salesman or even a salesman at all. He is merely a con man holding a salesman's title.

You are now moving into a sales role as you seek to influence stakeholders and earn their buy-in. A good way to start is to re-visit those stakeholders that you asked for advice when you were qualifying your goal. They are already familiar with what you want to accomplish and you have a head-start on building a positive relationship with them. Share with them the research that you did earlier that supports your case. Show sincerity and confidence. A little passion can go a long way but don't overdo it. Ask them for feedback. Do they believe you can achieve the goal? Are they willing to help? How much enthusiasm do they express? What do they see as obstacles for success? Do you need to speak with their superiors and would they be willing to broker a meeting?

This *bottoms up strategy* is a good one for buy-in. Work the prospective team members first before you go to their superiors. This can be done in one-on-one conversations or in group roundtable discussions depending on what you feel is most appropriate. When you are successful in convincing them, you will have a quorum that can have a positive snowballing effect on their management. Refer back to their individual interests in your goal and weave those points into your conversations. If they have objections, be patient and hear them out. They may raise points that you hadn't anticipated. Objections are an opportunity to strengthen your case. Tweak your presentation to address any missed points.

If prospective team members are currently working on an important project, find out when they expect to finish. Get a timeframe. Ask them about their manager's attitude. Solicit their opinions on how their manager might react to your request. Understand the manager's potential interests in your project and how you might influence him in a convincing way.

Once you have enough team members in the boat you will need to focus your sales efforts higher in your organization. That means connecting with the managers who have the authority to grant resources. Selling them on your goal will be much easier if you already have the buy-in and support from their individual team members.

Make sure your manager is involved and supports your efforts. Your manager can be a valuable resource for convincing peer or senior managers the critical importance your goal has for your organization.

There is no silver bullet in this early stage buy-in process. It takes preparation, integrity and conviction. You must believe in your goal and have confidence that you can achieve it. If you project this conviction in your delivery, your message will become contagious. You have many communication methods available to you that were discussed earlier in this chapter. Go with what you feel is most appropriate for each situation. Be comfortable with your own style and don't try to be someone else. You will find that your relationships will soon blossom and develop into trust and support.

To be successful, a man must exert an effective influence upon his brothers and upon his associates, and the degree in which he accomplishes this depends on the personality of the man. The incandescence of which he is capable. The flame of fire that burns inside of him. The magnetism which draws the heart of other men to him.

-Vince Lombardi

Chapter 4: Execution

Olympic athletes spend most of their lives practicing and preparing for the few seconds they will have to compete for a coveted world championship medal. Once a diver springs off the diving board or a figure skater takes to the ice, a judgement will be made on how well they performed. Their performance is about execution. The judges determine how well the athlete executed their particular routine.

Jack Welch is widely recognized as one of the most successful business leaders of our time. In a statement about leadership, he used the following words:

> *Good business leaders create a vision, articulate the vision, passionately own the vision, and relentlessly drive it to completion.*
>
> —Jack Welch

In Mr. Welch's statement, "relentlessly drive it to completion" is about execution.

Business execution is the process of getting something done within a reasonable timeframe. It is about achieving a goal and it is built upon a strategy and a plan. Without these two important elements, effective execution would be impossible. As I've stressed earlier in this book, up-front planning and preparation is critical for effective execution. Think back about how much time we spent preparing for this phase. It is now time for that preparation to pay off.

Execution can be divided into four activities as shown in Figure 5 below.

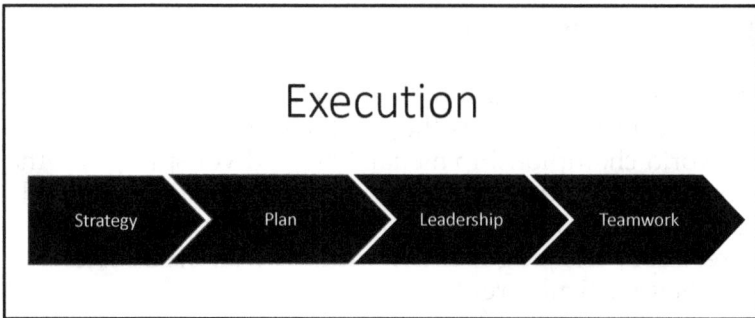

Figure 5 - Execution Phase

Strategy

Execution without a clear strategy is a recipe for failure. It can be expressed in a single paragraph or a few pages. Many times, strategy is confused with tactics. Here is a concise description of the differences:

> ...*tactics are the actual means used to gain an objective, while strategy is the overall campaign plan, which may involve complex operational patterns, activity, and decision-making that govern tactical execution*
>
> - Wikipedia

Consider Muhammad Ali's famous 1974 boxing match with George Foreman. Ali knew that Foreman had tremendous punching power and a good hit could result in a knock-out victory for him. Ali shrewdly adopted a strategy to win the fight. Instead of aggressively going after Foreman early in the fight and risking a knockout punch, he decided to wear Foreman down so that he would become exhausted. Once the fatigue set in on Foreman, Ali would gain the advantage and counter-punch his weakened opponent.

The tactics Ali used became known as the "Rope-a-Dope." Although this seems like a silly name, it was very effective. Ali first protected himself from Foreman's powerful blows by deflecting them as he held up his gloves in a heavily guarded position. As he did this, he leaned back against the ropes. Seeing the pummeling that Foreman was delivering, many spectators believed Ali was finished.

However, the ropes served as an elastic cushion and had a dampening effect on Foreman's punches. Had Ali not used the ropes, he would have absorbed the full impact of Foreman's blows thus degrading his ability to continue. As Forman continued to pound, he began to tire and let his guard down. Ali then took advantage of the opening and stepped up an offensive series of punches that won him the match.

This famous boxing match illustrates the difference between strategy and tactics. Ali's strategy was to wear his opponent down so he could avoid receiving a knock-out punch while creating an opening to deliver counter-punches of his own. The tactics he used were a shrewd combination of a guarded defensive position and the cushioning effects of the ropes.

A graphic representation of the relationship of strategy to tactics is show in Figure 6 below.

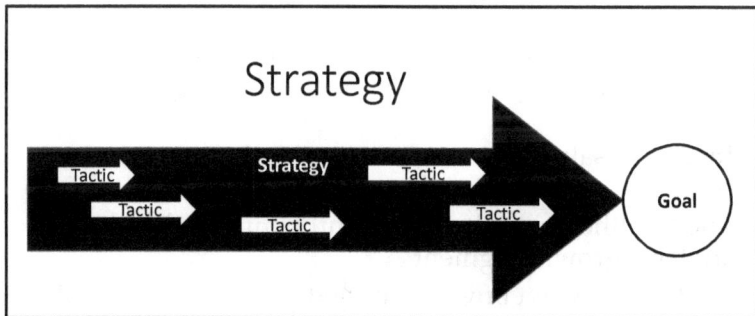

Figure 6 - Strategy

Think carefully about what your strategy is for achieving your goal. This shouldn't be difficult because in the earlier planning phases, you evaluated various different options that were candidates for your approach. You were looking for the best way to tackle the problem. The one you picked was what you felt was the best option. What were the reasons for the choice? Once you identify the key reasons, you can wrap them into a few simple sentences that will define your strategy.

Your strategy statement is a high-level declaration describing how you intend to achieve your objective. It is invaluable for building credibility both with prospective team members as well as the rest of the stakeholders. As mentioned earlier, many of the stakeholders won't read all of the detail in your documentation. However, most will read your strategy statement.

If you can't succinctly articulate a strategy, you will probably run into trouble maintaining support for your goal. Worse, you will probably have trouble accomplishing your goal. If you don't have clear strategy, your efforts won't be taken seriously and your goal will be nothing more than a pipe dream.

Keep in mind that strategy is not without risks. Stakeholders will understand that. After all, you are attempting to reach a stretch goal which is aggressive. To justify this, the goal payoff should exceed the perceived risks. Your strategy should provide a credible plan that is worth pursuing.

Let's go back and review our EMR certification example. The following are some snippets that define the challenge:

- Increased sales and margins are critical for your company's future growth
- The Healthcare market is currently untapped and is a strategic growth segment
- Customers won't buy an untested and uncertified EMR solution
- Your company doesn't have a tested and certified EMR solution
- Your company is losing sales to the competition who has a certified EMR solution
- The window of opportunity is six months

Now let's review the analysis you did that will form the basis of your Strategy statement:

- Engage a six-member cross-functional team of experts who are currently on-staff
- Perform testing in a local lab to maximize team availability and minimize travel costs
- Engage a Partner Alliance Engineer who will provide software for testing and final certification approval
- Achieve certification within the six-month window of opportunity
- Generate opportunity for rapid payback period with significant Return on Investment

We can now craft a compelling strategy statement which might look as follows:

> *My team will generate an opportunity to capture significant high margin sales by expanding into the strategic Healthcare market. This will be accomplished by providing a fully tested and certified EMR solution that will be competitive and attractive to prospective Healthcare customers.*

> *By engaging a six-member cross-functional team of experts who are currently on-staff, we will eliminate the need for outside hiring thus avoiding delays, added expense and risk. All testing will be performed in a local lab which will maximize team availability while minimizing travel expenses. A Partner Alliance Manager will provide the testing software which will eliminate the need for an expensive test bed.*

> *We will provide this solution within the six-month window of market opportunity with a rapid payback period and a significant return on investment.*

Plan

It is time to focus on the tactics that will get you to your goal in the stated timeframe. Think about the individual tasks that need to be accomplished and the order in which they need to be completed. How do they mesh to accomplish the overall objective? In this phase we will be using the terms *tactics* and *tasks* interchangeably. Remember, your tactics are the means for accomplishing your objective. They should support and be consistent with your strategy. For example, hiring a contract systems engineer would be inconsistent with your strategy of utilizing on-staff personnel.

It is possible to change your strategy in-flight but you should have a very good reason for doing this. It can be disruptive to the project and have a damaging effect on your credibility. If you decide to make changes to your communicated strategy without a very good rationale, you risk looking like you don't know what you are doing. Be careful. You've worked hard to build that credibility within your organization.

Tactics, on the other hand, may change several times over the course of your project. You may discover something along the way that you hadn't anticipated. This could justify or even necessitate a change in tactics. There could be a faster way of accomplishing a task or a better method to reduce cost or risk. Changing tactics in a fluid work environment is common.

External events may pop up that have an impact on your project. What if your lead performance engineer had a family emergency mid-project and had to leave town for a couple of weeks? How will you adjust? Can you accomplish what the performance engineer was tasked to do using backup personnel? Perhaps they will use a different approach but will still perform the task satisfactorily.

Some tasks will be dependent on the completion of earlier tasks before they can start. For example, EMR certification testing can't commence until the lab test bed is fully configured. Without a configured test bed, you'd have nothing to test on. Those are two individual tasks but they are linked by a dependency.

Tasks that don't have dependency linkages are candidates for concurrent execution although their timing should make sense. Ongoing communication of the project's current status to stakeholders can be done while testing is underway. Frequent communication keeps the scope of your efforts in front of the stakeholders and gives them a sense of involvement. This serves to enhance your credibility and boosts their trust in your leadership.

You aren't expected to develop the plan in a vacuum. Collaborate with your team members and get their input on the tasks that need to be accomplished. This is a good opportunity to further develop and solidify your relationships with the team members. They will appreciate your willingness to include them and that you value their input. A roundtable discussion with an accompanying whiteboard is a good way to do this. You can hand the whiteboard marker to your team members where appropriate to further gain their input and involvement.

Understand the linkages between tasks and weigh the different options. What are the risks with each approach? Which tactics have the best chances for success? Do all tasks support the goal? Can you streamline the project by eliminating any unnecessary tasks? Get everyone's input and opinions. Get consensus where you can on the best approaches. Give credit to the team members who originated the tactical ideas you decide to employ.

In this phase you may want to engage the services of a professional Project Manager within your organization. A project manager's primary role is to keep the project on-track and to periodically report the status to the stakeholders. If you team with a competent project manager, a lot of the burden of the routine project management effort can be offloaded. You will still need to stay involved and participate in the regular status meetings. Keep in mind that you own the project and the project manager is merely keeping this phase of your overall path to your goal on-track.

Whether you decide to engage the services of a professional project manager or manage this phase yourself, you should be familiar with some of the common terminology and tools used in project management.

Project Management Terms

The following is a sampling of some of the common project management terms.[1]

Mission Statement – A concise statement, usually one paragraph, summarizing what the project is about and what it will accomplish.

Assumptions – Factors that, for planning purpose, are considered to be true or certain without proof or demonstration.

Level of Effort (LOE) – The number of labor units required to complete an activity or other project element. Usually expressed as staff hours, staff days or staff weeks. Should not be confused with duration.

Duration – The amount of time to complete a specific task given other commitments, work, vacations, etc. Usually expressed as workdays or workweeks.

Task – A well-defined component of project work.

Activity – The work or effort needed to achieve a result. An activity consumes time and usually consumes resources.

Statement of Work (SOW) – A narrative description of products or services required for successful completion of the project.

---

[1] Source: State of Michigan Department of Technology, Management & Budget – Project Management Key Terms.

Deliverable – Any measurable, tangible, verifiable outcome, result or item that must be produced to complete a project.

Project Plan – A formal approved document used to guide both project execution and project control. The primary uses of the Project Plan are to document planning, assumptions and decisions, facilitate the communication among Stakeholders and document approved scope, cost and schedule.

Critical Success Factors – Identified factors that must be present in order for the project to be successful in terms of scope/budget/schedule.

Scope – The sum of the products and services to be provided as a project.

Scope Creep – The gradual addition of new requirements to the original product definitions. Usually to be avoided.

Change Control – A change in objectives, work plan, or schedule resulting in a material difference from the terms of previously granted approval to proceed.

Contingency – An event that may happen in the future such as a problem, emergency or expense that might arise unexpectedly and must be prepared for. A provision made against future unforeseen events.

Workaround – A response to a negative risk event. It is distinguished from a continency plan in that a workaround is not planned in advance of the occurrence of the risk event.

Schedule – The planned dates for performing activities and for meeting deliverables.

Critical Path – The sequence of tasks that determine the minimum schedule for a project. If one task on the critical path is delayed, the schedule will be late.

Milestone – A significant event in the project that is usually a completion of a major deliverable.

Acceptance Criteria – Those criteria, that includes deliverables, performance requirements and essential conditions which must be met to complete project deliverables and be accepted.

Status Report - A report containing information on a specific project indicating if the project is ahead of schedule, on schedule or behind schedule relative to the project plan.

Gantt Chart – A graphic display of coordinated schedule related information. In the typical bar chart, schedule activities or work breakdown structure components are listed down the left side of the chart, dates are shown across the top, and activity durations are shown as date-placed horizontal bars. An example is shown in Figure 7 below.[2]

ID	Task Name	Predecessors	Duration
1	Start		0 days
2	a	1	4 days
3	b	1	5.33 days
4	c	2	5.17 days
5	d	2	6.33 days
6	e	3,4	5.17 days
7	f	5	4.5 days
8	g	6	5.17 days
9	Finish	7,8	0 days

Figure 7 - Gantt Chart

Tracking Tools

Microsoft Project is a widely-used software package for project tracking and reporting. It only runs on the Windows operating system but there are equivalent software packages available for Mac OS. If you decide to manage the project yourself, strongly consider using one of these packages. Virtually all professional Project Managers use one of these tools.

Leadership

---

[2] Source: Wikipedia

We have been discussing a framework for effective leadership throughout this book. Most of the elements thus far have been analytical in nature. Because of this, they are often overlooked or simply avoided. These early stages of analysis and preparation are necessary because they enable and set the stage for the effective application of the interpersonal traits more commonly associated with leadership. These are the traits and techniques the leader uses to influence the team to sign on and aggressively pursue the goal.

Leadership is often confused with management. Have you ever heard the aspiring college graduate say that their career goal is to "get into management?" Do they really want to be a manager or do they want to be a leader? The two are not synonymous. Do they know the difference and can they articulate it? I would conjecture that many cannot.

The following is one of the best delineations I have seen:

> *Management is the allocation of scarce resources against an organization's objective, the setting of priorities, the design of work and the achievement of results. Most important, it is about controlling.*

> *Leadership, on the other hand, focuses on the creation of a common vision. It means motivating people to contribute to the vision and encouraging them to align their self-interest with that of the organization. It means persuading, not commanding.*

> George B. Weathersby
> Former President and CEO
> American Management Association

Does Mr. Weathersby's description of leadership sound familiar? Can you see its difference from management? This is exactly what we are striving to do as we move along the path to our goal!

Let's take a closer look into the traits inherent in a successful leader. Many business books have been written on the subject.

Leadership Traits

When you think of major organizations that have earned a reputation for excellence in execution what comes to mind? There are many business organizations that have been very successful due to sound leadership and extraordinary execution. IBM, General Electric, Apple and Ford are just a few examples and entire books have been written about them. In these cases, the discussion centered around the actions taken by their leaders that contributed to their organization's success.

One organization that consistently earns a reputation for execution excellence is the U.S Marine Corps. The Marines are known for accomplishing their mission in spite of very challenging odds. In countless situations the Marines have been called upon first, before other forces arrive to join them.

The U.S. Marine Corps efficiency is attributed to extraordinary training and discipline. I served in The Marine Corps and can attest to the fact that this is instilled in every Marine through an uncompromising leadership regimen.

There is much we can learn from the Marine Corps ethos and leadership principles. Although the Marine Corps is a military organization, its leadership principles are equally applicable to the business world. It is worth taking a look at these and assessing how well you meet these criteria. Have you overlooked any? Is there room for improvement? If you are strong on all points, you are doing extremely well. The following is a summary of them. For the few references that are Marine Corps specific, I have made annotations in parenthesis noting their application to business teams.[3]

---

[3] Source: Leadership Guide, Lejeune Leadership Institute, U.S. Marine Corps Base, Quantico, VA

Integrity – Uprightness of character and soundness of moral principle, absolute truthfulness and honesty.

Knowledge – Acquired information, including professional knowledge and an understanding of your Marines (your team).

Courage – A mental quality that recognizes fear of danger or criticism but enables one to proceed in the face of it with calmness and firmness.

Decisiveness – Ability to reach decisions promptly and to announce them in a clear and forceful manner.

Dependability – The certainty of the proper performance of duty.

Initiative – Seeing what has to be done and commencing on a course of action, even in the absence of orders.

Tact – The ability to deal with others without creating offence.

Justice – The quality of being impartial and consistent in exercising command.

Enthusiasm – The display of sincere interest and exuberance in the performance of duty.

Bearing – Creating a favorable impression in carriage, appearance and personal conduct at all times.

Endurance – The mental and physical stamina measure by the ability to stand pain, fatigue, distress and hardship.

Unselfishness – Avoidance of providing for one's comfort and personal advancement at the expense of others.

Loyalty – Faithfulness to Country, Corps, Unit and to your seniors and subordinates (your organization and your team).

Judgement – The quality of weighing facts and possible solutions on which to base decisions.

Tips and Techniques

The following are some tips on leadership that you might find helpful as you move through the Execution phase.

Regular Communication

It is important to keep the stakeholders informed on your progress on a regular basis. This is usually done on a weekly schedule but you might find bi-weekly calls more appropriate. Stakeholders are usually very busy with competing demands on their time. They tend to pursue other interests and can potentially forget about your activities. By communicating with them on a regular basis you keep them informed and engaged which is critical for their ongoing support.

No Bloated Time Wasters

Keep your communications on point and avoid wandering off topic. Some small talk at the beginning of the meeting is appropriate but don't let the meeting turn into a participant's fifteen-minute monologue about their recent camping trip or vacation in Bermuda. These are good conversations to have for developing personal relationships. However, they are time wasters during a status call.

Save these conversations for lunchtime, a coffee break or a drink after work. Participants in your meetings will appreciate that you value their time and will usually make a point to attend in the future.

Start your meeting or call promptly and end it on-time or before. Don't try to fill up your timeslot if there is nothing more to say. Participants always appreciate an early release. Avoid meetings or calls that extend beyond the allotted timeslot. Extending a call or meeting can cause your participants to be late for their next meeting. Many will be uncomfortable with their tardiness and will regard it as reflection of your lack of planning. A better approach is to allow enough time for your meeting and give some time back if you don't need the entire timeslot.

Get Feedback

Solicit feedback from your team members on a regular basis. Is there a better tactic or more efficient way to move along the path to success? How do they view the progress? This is a good opportunity to take their temperature and see how they are feeling. Are they still bought-in and enthusiastic? If not, try to address their concerns. If you can't address their issues immediately, take notes and follow up in a subsequent meeting. Never ignore a valid concern.

Many times, participants will be reluctant to volunteer comments especially in a large group setting. In these cases, you may need to query them. Going around the table and asking each participant for input is a good way to do this. That way you are not perceived as singling anyone out. Do it in a tactful way and avoid putting anyone on the spot. If someone has nothing to say or add, don't make a big deal about it and move on. Always show appreciation for their feedback even if you don't necessarily agree with it.

Filter Out

A particularly valuable skill is the ability to ingest a large volume of information and filter out the points that are not important or relevant to achieving your goal. By doing this, you can focus on the important points, make informed decisions and take rational actions.

This is not always easy to do and takes discipline. Wasting time on irrelevant information is an invitation for important factors to become de-emphasized or ignored. This can result in your project going off the rails. When receiving new information, you should always be asking "is this important and relevant to my objective."

If not, take a quick note of it for future consideration as circumstances could change. In these cases, you will have a brief record to which you can refer to and revisit if any points later rise in importance. Concentrate your time and effort on the information that has a direct impact on the success of your project. Filter out the rest.

Tracking Progress

If you engaged the services of a professional project manager, most of this effort can be offloaded to that person. If not, you'll need to track the project yourself. A software tool such as Microsoft Project is invaluable for organizing and reporting project status information. This includes tracking costs, variances, critical path activities and other key metrics. If you have never managed a project, project management software can provide organization that will make your job a lot easier.

Dealing with Setbacks

Any complex project has inherent risks and associated setbacks. A setback is an event that has a negative effect on the foreword movement of the project. Examples are a key team member getting sick, an unexpected snowstorm that prevents the team from working, a delay in the shipment of equipment or a power failure in a test lab.

To keep your project moving, you'll probably need to deal with setbacks. You'll first need to assess whether the setback has a major or negligible impact on the project. If it is negligible, you should be able to proceed without any significant corrective action.

If the setback is major, you'll need to search for an alternative course of action or *workaround*. For example, you may have anticipated the possibility of a setback such as a team member getting sick. As a result, you established a contingency plan. In the Planning phase you identified alternate team members who might not have been your primary choices but nevertheless could fulfill a vacant role satisfactorily. You'll just need to check on their availability as your project is now in-flight.

In other cases, you need to use your creative abilities in identifying and implementing a workaround. You are encouraged to draw upon the input from your team for ideas and feasibility.

The extent to which you can identify and implement effective workarounds when setbacks arise can be the difference between success and failure. A setback can delay your target completion date. Is this acceptable? What is the tolerance for pushing the completion date further out? How would this affect the availability of the team members? Will market opportunities be lost or significantly diluted if you deliver late? These are some of the issues you will grapple with in dealing with setbacks.

The best way to minimize the negative effects of setbacks is to anticipate them in the early stages of planning and establish contingency plans. For unanticipated setbacks, be creative and reassuring as you identify and implement the best possible workarounds. By doing this, you will maintain the momentum and your project will continue moving in a forward direction.

Patience versus Push

Have ever heard the expression "I've fallen and I can't get up!"[4] The origin of this expression was a 1980's television commercial. It depicted an elderly woman who had fallen to a bathroom floor and was in need of emergency assistance. She uttered this statement and then depressed a button on a transmitting device that summoned help. LifeCall, the commercial's sponsor was promoting their transmitting pendant and emergency services.

Since the release of the commercial, this expression has been turned upside down to describe the opposite of the original intention – that of a person who is making illegitimate excuses for not being able to perform a task. You have probably known

---

[4] Registered trademark of Life Alert Emergency Response, Inc.

someone who lacked confidence to perform or was downright lazy. They probably fit this description.

As a leader you may face times when team members will complain about not being able to fulfill their duties. You will need to sort out whether the objections are legitimate or merely excuses. If you have chosen a competent and professional team, you will probably not encounter many illegitimate excuses.

Occasionally, a team member may offer up an objection for why he can't perform his assigned task. You will need to be tactful as you probe and make an assessment to the legitimacy of his argument. Before you start, you should *always* assume his reasoning is legitimate. Like an innocent man condemned to prison, it is far worst to dismiss a legitimate objection than it is to accept an illegitimate excuse. Exercise patience while you investigate.

Work through the issue with the team member. Ask him what he needs to complete the task. If he says he needs help and you can provide it without undue stress or added cost, give him the benefit of the doubt and get him what he needs. This is especially true for marginal cases where you are unable to come to a clear-cut conclusion. You may find that when he realizes you are willing to work with him, he will be more willing to work with you.

However, if the team member falls into a pattern of repeated excuses with limited or no performance, you will need to put your foot down. Be firm but reasonable and don't lose your temper. Explain to him that you think he can accomplish the task if he puts his mind to it. Offer him encouragement and try to keep the discussion on a positive keel. You will need to push on him a bit but be sure to express confidence in his abilities. After all, you picked him for your team for a reason. If you are successful in turning his attitude around, you may find he will later thank you. He may have "fallen" but you "helped him get up."

Barry McGuire sang a #1 hit song at the height of the Cold War with the Soviet Union called *The Eve of Destruction*.[5] The song described the potential devastating effects of a nuclear war between the two world superpowers.

An excerpt of the lyrics of the song are as follows:

> *If the button is pushed, there's no running away,*
> *There'll be no one to save with the world in a grave...*

I was in my teens when this song was released and it created a lasting impression on me. The melody rang out so simply and so beautifully but at the same time the lyrics painted a dire picture of society's dysfunction and the potential to end the World. McGuire's gravelly voice struck an unmistakable note of urgency and he was very pointed in delivering his passionate message.

Mr. McGuire was describing the original meaning of the Nuclear Option, that of Nuclear War between nuclear armed nations. The term has since been applied to less consequential but nevertheless significant actions taken by members of the United States Congress and various business leaders.

In the business world the nuclear option is a drastic action taken to achieve a goal. It is usually an act of desperation and last resort when all other approaches have failed. An example of the nuclear option is going to a team member's boss and revealing how he is underperforming. You ask his boss for help in correcting his behavior. Although this approach may work in the short run, it can have a devastating effect on your future relationship with that team member, other team members and possibly his boss. It may result in an unwinnable situation for all parties as Barry McGuire pointed out in his song. Be careful with this.

---

[5] *The Eve of Destruction* was written by P.F. Sloan who, among others also performed it.

However, there may be times when the nuclear option is your only choice. You may be very close to achieving your goal but the lynchpin is stubbornly standing in the way. If you have exhausted all other more positive approaches, it might be time to execute your last resort in the final push to your goal.

The general rule is to avoid this option and aggressively look for better alternatives. You will need to be very careful with this as it has the potential to create a damaging affect for all parties and their future relationships. Strive for win-win tactics as you execute your strategy. This is always your preferred course of action.

The Light at the End of the Tunnel

Some of the longest train tunnels in the World are located in Europe. The famous Channel Tunnel that connects The United Kingdom with France is 31 miles long. As a train speeds through the tunnel, its passengers rely on the train's electro-mechanical systems along with the engineer's judgement to safely transport them to the opposite end and on to their destination.

As the train progresses through the darkness of the tunnel, the operating engineers and some of the passengers view an expanding dot of light emanating from the tunnel exit. This is a visual indication that the tunnel segment of their journey is almost over. From examples such as this, the expression "seeing the light at the end of the tunnel" was born.

It is not uncommon for a few passengers to feel some anxiety while traveling through a tunnel especially when they know they are deep below the ocean floor or inside a mountain. Some people can feel claustrophobic. They know that they are traveling at the mercy of the engineering competence that went into building the tunnel. Their anxieties are then tamped down as the reassuring light emerges in the distance.

You may be wondering what relevance this has to achieving a goal. Some team members can develop second doubts about whether the goal is truly achievable. This can be the result of several factors including working long hours, exhaustion or witnessing multiple setbacks. This is especially prevalent in long engagements where the goal is particularly aggressive.

It is your job as a leader to reassure the team that the goal is still within reach and that they are closing in on the objective. The "light at the end of the tunnel" is within view and the illuminating dot is expanding.

Be honest and forthright about this and don't sugarcoat it. Point out the major milestones the team has already accomplished and contrast these with the ones that remain. Go over what is left to be done and how and when the team will push over the finish line. Express confidence in the abilities of your team and it's individual members. Offer encouragement. Strive to keep their morale at the highest possible level. Be empathetic but dispense with any negative distractions.

Avoiding the Endless Loop

Early in my career I worked as an operations research analyst for a commercial bank. A large part of my job involved writing computer programs in the FORTRAN programming language. In those early days of computing, I'd sit at a card punch machine and type in each computer instruction, one per card. When I was done, I would submit the card deck to a computer operator who would feed it into a massive IBM 370 mainframe computer for execution.

I'd usually have to wait a few hours before the results would be returned. They were printed on green bar paper which was ejected from a large line printer. One day I had the misfortune of submitting a program with a bug that produced an endless loop. My computer instructions would execute serially until one pernicious instruction would jump to the beginning of the sequence and start it all over again. The program would loop and loop and never finish.

The computer operator left my program running for several minutes until he realized it was probably stuck in an endless loop. He eventually terminated it using commands issued from his control console. This was seen as a tremendous waste of expensive computer resources. I have to admit that computer operator was not particularly fond of me after that incident. I later corrected the bug and my program produced some valuable information for the bank. I learned from this experience to be more careful in my coding and to avoid "the endless loop."

Like a computer program stuck in an endless loop or a cat chasing its tail, some projects tend to spin out of control just before the goal is reached. A lot of time is spent doing additional work that wasn't part of the original scope. The project continues to spin and slips past the projected end date. It seems to go on forever and saps the team's energy and enthusiasm. This can be caused by scope creep or the lack of a clear definition of the goal. Recall the importance of knowing your target. If the target is vague, it can be subject to interpretation or misunderstood altogether.

You've planned for this and spent considerable time documenting your objective. You can now use that documentation to remind anyone who has forgotten or has second-thoughts about what your objective really is. When you have clear-cut documentation as a reference point, it is much easier to declare that the goal has been achieved. At that critical juncture, you will need to drive a stake in the ground and declare victory. You can then state that it is time to move on.

Teamwork

Every year The Boston Pops Orchestra performs a free concert on the banks of the Charles River to celebrate America's Independence Day. Tens of thousands of patriotic concertgoers flood the grassy esplanade in hopes of securing a good spot for their picnic blanket or folding chairs.

True to their name, The Pops perform popular songs from composers and lyricists such as Katherine Lee Bates, Francis Scott Key, Samuel Francis Smith, Julia Ward Howe and others. Although these names may not be familiar, their songs are very well known -- *America the Beautiful, The Star-Spangled Banner, My Country 'Tis of Thee and The Battle Hymn of the Republic.*

Traditionally, the concert culminates with the playing of Tchaikovsky's 1812 Overture. This is a bit curious because Tchaikovsky wasn't an American. He was Russian and wrote this overture to commemorate Russia's defense of its homeland against Napoleon's invading forces. Therein lies the parallel with America's fight for independence and its celebration on July 4th.

Beyond its origin however, the 1812 Overture is a powerful instrumental masterpiece. It starts slowly and eventually builds to a crescendo that finishes with a brass fanfare finale, church chimes and cannon fire. It is always a crowd pleaser and it is no wonder that it is chosen as the signature performance of the celebration.

A professional orchestra such as The Boston Pops is a good example of closely coordinated teamwork. Its ninety or so musicians play their instruments at just the right time, at the right tempo and the with right accent to produce a beautiful musical performance.

The conductor is the leader who coordinates the actions of the players. Without the conductor, there would be discord and a pleasing performance would be impossible. The conductor is the enabler of their teamwork.

Like an orchestra, your team are the "musicians" and you are the "conductor." You will be coordinating their efforts to produce a successful team outcome. Like a musical score, a carefully documented plan will be your guide.

Each player has specialized skills that they can contribute. As the team's leader, it is improbable that you will have deeper skills than that held by each player in their respective roles. They are specialists and are the experts of their roles on the team. Don't tell them how to do their job. Tell them what needs to be done and let them figure out how to do it. Nobody likes a micro-manager and a good leader will avoid this. Think "coordination", not "micro-management."

> *The best leader is the one who has sense enough to pick good men to do what he wants done, and the self-restraint to keep from meddling with them while they do it.*

-Theodore Roosevelt

Chapter 5: The Buy-in Magnet

You are now in the final stretch. You've exercised considerable discipline and have been thorough in your planning. You gained the support of the stakeholders and assembled a winning team. You motivated the team and avoided the common pitfalls. Your strategy and execution have paid off as you close in on the final push to your goal.

Once you cross the finish line, your team will have a great sense of accomplishment and some well-deserved relief. They will take pride in having been part of a winning team and will have respect for your leadership abilities. In the back of their minds they know they will soon be released to pursue other activities. At this point you are well on your way to creating the Buy-in Magnet. However, you are not there yet. There are still some critically important activities that need to be addressed.

By now you are very close to achieving your goal. However, just reaching your goal is not enough. This chapter discusses what's left to be done in achieving a more powerful and far reaching goal – one that has not been discussed yet. The pursuit of this secondary but significant goal is known as *Creating the Buy-in Magnet*.

There are four remaining activities in The Buy-in Magnet phase as shown in Figure 8 below. Although there is a natural tendency to gloss over or omit these activities altogether, don't fall victim to this common mistake. Without a strong finish, you may be successful in accomplishing your primary goal but you run the risk of it devolving into a vague and distant memory. In that case, the Buy-in Magnet would be lost. Don't let this happen. Stay focused and keep the pressure on. Grab for two brass rings, not just one.

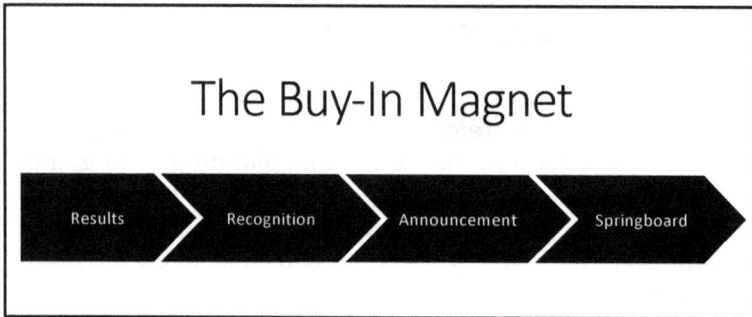

The Buy-In Magnet

Results > Recognition > Announcement > Springboard

Figure 8 - The Buy-in Magnet Phase

Results

Results are the fruit of your team's labor. If you reached your goal, the results will usually bear this out and speak for themselves. However, in the fast-pasted frensy of the business world, even good results can be lost. To illustrate this let's return for one last time to our Electronic Medical Records (EMR) certification testing example.

Avoid the Nightmare Scenario

Recall that the goal was to reach 5,000 transactions per second on a specific set of servers, networking and storage. It was to be accomplished within a six-month period and a validation would be provided by the Partner Alliance Manager who was providing the software. This certification would indicate that the joint solution would perform well and meet customers' expectations.

Once the certification was achieved, your company could provide a viable EMR infrastructure solution and would expand its reach into the lucrative Healthcare market. As you pointed out earlier, this would generate significant returns in both top-line revenue and healthy margins.

Over the past five months, your team has been busy testing and tuning the infrastructure configuration for optimum results. The day has finally arrived to invite the Partner Alliance Manager to observe the 5,000+ transactions per second your team is able to demonstrate. He's impressed, gives a thumbs up and you think you have achieved your goal. Everyone is enthusiastic.

A week later you find that routine phone calls you placed to the Partner Alliance Manager haven't been returned. You then call the front desk and learn that he has since left the company. At the time this doesn't seem like a major issue because it happens all the time in this industry.

Meanwhile, your company's sales force is ecstatic about having a new solution offering for the Healthcare market. During a sales call one of your top sales representatives finds that her prospective customer is concerned whether the solution she is offering has been certified. On your advice she states to them that the solution was fully tested and certified by the EMR software company.

The prospective customer then calls the EMR software company to validate her claim. The company states they don't have any knowledge or record of a certification. Your sales representative becomes upset and questions your credibility. She then abandons her sales campaign.

You then pursue the Partner Alliance Manager who gave you the thumbs up. Upon further investigation you find that he has joined one of your principle competitors and apparently has no interest in validating your claim. He doesn't return your calls and you don't even get a chance to speak with him. Any hope for concrete proof of the certification has vanished. Your worst nightmare has occurred.

Get It in Writing

The importance of having a disciplined approach to documentation cannot be overstated. In the above circumstance, the absence of a written record of the certification has scuttled the goal. Don't let this happen to you! Once you have achieved your goal, strive to get a formal written declaration of completion from the appropriate authority. This will serve as concrete proof that you accomplished your mission.

In the above example, a simple email sent from the Partner Alliance Manager to you would have been sufficient. It should have been drafted during or shortly after the certification test was observed. The email should state with specificity what was accomplished and who observed it. As with most emails, it would automatically show current time and date stamps. The use of the word *certifies* would have been appropriate to make certain the intention of the message was clear.

This would provide concrete proof of the certification to prospective customers. It also would serve as a credible communication vehicle to inform members of the EMR software company who were not aware of the certification.

You may find that some authorities will procrastinate or be reluctant to sign off on your accomplishment. They may not be comfortable with a written expression or they may just have trouble making a simple decision. In these cases, you may want to draft the email yourself. That way you make it easy for them as they can just cut and paste your text and email it you. You can also draft it in advance so you'll have it ready when you need it. Don't let them off the hook. You've earned it and don't deserve the potential for a "nightmare scenario."

Recognition

One of the most disturbing practices found in the business world is the grandstanding business leader who takes full credit for someone else's work. He might steal a great idea and call it his own or omit giving credit to the team members who helped achieve a goal. Unfortunately, this is an all too common practice. Although the leader who exhibits this unethical behavior might advance his standing in the short-term, he poisons any goodwill he might have previously developed with the victims of his disingenuous behavior.

As a kid I had a matchbox-sized toy that consisted of two plastic terrier dogs mounted on bar magnets. When the dogs were moved toward one another, they would either be attracted or repelled, depending on their relative positions and the polarity of the magnets. Like the toy dogs, I can't help but think how the unethical business leader put his "magnet" in the wrong position and repelled those around him. Good luck to him for any future buy-in!

A critical part of creating the Buy-in Magnet is giving honest and substantive recognition to those who deserve it. This goes beyond the common lip service of a "mention" when running down a list of contributors. It involves putting some thought into what each team member contributed.

Where possible, focus on their unique abilities and strengths. You may find someone likeable but popularity is a poor substitute for professional achievement recognition. Imagine you are writing their yearly performance review. What strengths did they bring to the team and how did they apply them in achieving the goal? Be honest but not patronizing. You should be able to express this in one or two paragraphs. Make sure you document it.

Once you have a record of each player's contributions, convey your thoughts to those people who have an interest in their standing, including advancement and promotions. An obvious place to start is their immediate superiors. Visit or call each manager and express thanks for offering their services and participation on your team. State that you accomplished your objective and include your comments about how their player contributed to the team's success.

Follow up with a brief email to each manager re-iterating your thanks and your summary thoughts. They will then have a written record to draw upon when the time comes for the player's yearly performance review. They may even choose a "cut and paste" operation which will make their job easier at review time.

Through this minimal effort, you will be developing allies not only with each team player but with their managers as well. This will make it easier to get their buy-in for your next endeavor, should you need their services again. It will also have a positive affect throughout the organization as word spreads of your accomplishment and the recognition you gave to your team.

Announcement

You've been in regular communication with your immediate stakeholders and team members and they all know that you have accomplished your mission. They also recognize its significance. However, there are other people in your organization that might have an interest in knowing about your achievement.

This is the second tier of communication that is targeted at a much wider audience. This activity is optional and will depend on the nature of your achievement. If you accomplished a stretch goal that has significant and wide-reaching benefits, it is probably worthy of an announcement. Most employees have an interest in developments that have a positive impact on the success of their organization. You will need to decide if making an announcement is appropriate or not.

There are some fundamental reasons why you should consider proceeding in this vein. First, you will be taking your message directly to your organization. By doing so, you will eliminate the filtering and spin that commonly occurs through word of mouth communication. Second, you will minimize the possibility that your message will be marginalized or lost altogether. Third, you will short-circuit any unscrupulous actions made by bad actors in their attempts to usurp credit for your achievement. You and your team worked hard for this and deserve the recognition. By making an announcement, The Buy-in Magnet casts a wider net and is further strengthened in the process.

The announcement can be made using a variety of communication methods. The simplest form is a carefully crafted email sent to a larger group, beyond the nucleus of your original stakeholders. It can be sent to a department, a division or to your entire company. You should get honest advice from several stakeholders before deciding how wide the distribution should be. Above, all make sure the announcement is relevant and of interest to your audience. Sending an email to a company-wide email distribution carries the risk of being perceived as grandstanding. Give this some careful thought before proceeding.

Be brief but include content drawn from material you developed earlier. State what you accomplished, why it is important to the organization, who was involved and any other material you feel is of interest and relevant. Any more than a few paragraphs of this too much. An effective technique is to include hyper-links to additional on-line material for those that want more detail. This material could include a data sheet, an in-depth whitepaper, a PowerPoint presentation, a "cheat sheet" or any other documents you feel would be useful to your audience.

Other examples of effective communications include conference calls, webinars, press releases and participation in division-wide team meetings. You may think of others. The type of communication will be highly dependent on the audience you wish to reach and the desired timing of the message. Some opportunities require scheduling well in advance. Others can be done immediately. You will need to decide which communications are most appropriate for your situation. Keep in mind that messages intended for audiences outside your organization should receive prior approval from your legal or marketing authorities.

Springboard

If you followed the framework provided in this book this far you probably created the Buy-in Magnet. Congratulations! At this point, you may wonder "What exactly is the Buy-in Magnet?" Let's take a closer look.

The Buy-in Magnet is an elevated state of professional standing within the business community. It is the achievement of a secondary and more far-reaching goal than the original stretch goal. The Buy-in Magnet is a strong recognition of your leadership abilities by those around you. Like a real magnet, it creates a force field that attracts co-workers to your cause. Going forward they will be more likely to accept your vision and voluntarily sign on to your mission.

The Buy-in Magnet is about earning respect by accepting a challenging goal and leading a cross-functional team to success. It's about beating the odds through discipline, organization and effective communication. It's about fairness and the way you treat other people in spite of pressure and adversity. The Buy-in Magnet is never "a given" and is always earned. It takes preparation, hard work, tact and good judgement. Above all it takes a burning desire to succeed.

Now that you have achieved the Buy-in Magnet, you may ask "What's next?" Most independent business consultants are always on the lookout for their next engagement. Near the end of their current engagement they usually spend more time sizing up future business opportunities. Successful consultants usually secure their next engagement with minimal downtime. Others struggle and experience costly gaps in their employment.

Like a gymnast who uses a springboard to propel her high into the air for maximum performance, the Buy-in Magnet is your springboard to your next opportunity. You've created the credibility that will make stakeholder buy-in much easier in your second round. They will be impressed with your track record and will be more willing to grant you the resources you need. Team members will be more willing to step up and volunteer their services as they will be eager to join a winning team.

You've accomplished your mission and it's time to look for your next "Moonshot" opportunity. There are many out there waiting to be discovered. The field of leadership will be sparse as others will shy away and be content with slam dunk opportunities. For them, mediocrity is an acceptable paradigm. As you circle back and evaluate the enormous contributions you can make for your organization, you think about what lies ahead. You have confidence that you can lead a cross-function team again to achieve extraordinary success. Moreover, your organization has confidence in *you* because you have created the Buy-in Magnet.

> *The greatest leader is not necessarily the one who does the greatest things. He is the one that gets the people to do the greatest things.*
>
> --Ronald Reagan

Chapter 6: Final Comments

Golden Nuggets

Over the course of my career I appreciated the learning opportunities that my employers afforded me. This included sales and technical training, ethics, contract law, finance and a variety of others.

I often heard my colleagues express their misgivings about this training by saying "I already know all that stuff." I understood their sentiment but never fully agreed with it. I always took advantage of the training that was available to me and read the business books that my leadership had provided. I never wrote off any as a useless exercise.

As I gained more experience and knowledge, some of the material seemed redundant and elementary to me. However, my rewards came as "golden nuggets" that were buried deep in the material. These were the new thoughts and fresh ideas that I hadn't previous considered. At a minimum, I walked away with at least a few valuable insights. More often, I learned a lot from the material that was provided. My training and reading efforts proved worthwhile as I continued to expand my knowledge and increase my value to the organization.

If you finished reading *Creating the Buy-in Magnet*, you probably have the same appetite for the learning that I described. Learning is a continuous process and should not stop when you stowed your graduation cap and gown. Experience is probably the best teacher but training and reading are not far behind. I urge you to continue taking advantage of these opportunities.

The Right Things

One sunny afternoon I was standing on a sidewalk having conversation with a peer co-worker of mine. We were on the same business team and had just finished having lunch together.

We had been discussing a go-forward plan for our afternoon business activities. My co-worker made a statement that I will always remember. In the course of the conversation he said "We need to make our boss look good."

This caught me by surprise. My principle reason for signing on to our boss's team was not to make him look good. I was there to do a job and do it well. However, I didn't have grievances regarding my boss and genuinely wished him well.

I realized that if I made significant contributions to his team, my boss would benefit from my successes. My focus was directed squarely at my goals and I knew that if I was successful, the rest would fall into place. Everyone would win.

At times employees fall into the trap of getting sidetracked in trying to please their superiors. They spend an inordinate amount of time crafting PowerPoint presentations meant to impress. In the process they take their eye off more important activities. This unproductive behavior has a corrosive effect on the considerable effort needed to reach a stretch goal.

Don't make the mistake of becoming ensnared in this trap. It can sap your time and energy that can result in a disappointing shortfall. Focus on what's truly important, do the right things and always reach for your goals. Stay focused and you will find that everything else will fall into place. Your boss and your peers will applaud your accomplishments.

Have Fun

We all spend roughly a third of our working lives doing our jobs. A third is probably a low estimate when you factor in working late, travel and trips away from home. What a dull and boring existence we would have if we never had any fun during our hours of employment.

Many employers recognize the importance of this and sponsor events designed to address employee satisfaction. These events might include a lunchtime barbecue, an interdepartmental softball game or an ice cream social. These are usually sprinkled in and around your normal workday grind.

More importantly, your job itself should provide some enjoyment and satisfaction. Although a "perfect job" is rare, the degree of happiness you experience can have a direct bearing on your performance. If you hate your job, you probably aren't living up to the performance level you are capable of. That could mean a discouraging miss on a critical goal.

Consider making a yearly evaluation of your past year work experience. Remove any emotion and be honest and objective. Overall, are you enjoying your work? Are you having some fun in the process? Hopefully you will be able to answer in the affirmative. If not, it may be time to move on to another job opportunity where you can fully exploit the potential of your capabilities.

Extend a Helping Hand

When I was in my early teens I advanced from building things from wood such as my kayak to go-karts and other metalworking crafts. One of my projects involved building a motorized bicycle made from junk parts I scavenged from our local transfer station.

Along the way I acquired an oxy-acetylene welding torch. I never had any formal instruction on how to use it so I picked up a book that described its operation. Most of the instruction was straightforward and easy to understand. However, there was one critical part that wasn't clear to me. The book described a *neutral flame* that is used when welding steel because it doesn't produce undesirable oxides in the welded material.

I understood the concept but had a difficult time internalizing the book's black and white photograph of the flame. Adjusting the torch to produce this type of flame was another enigma. Therefore, I set out to get some experienced advice.

I returned to the shop where I had purchased the torch a few weeks earlier. There were two salesmen seated behind the counter. They were wearing polo shirts that had their company logo and first names embroidered on the pockets. I asked one of them how I could adjust my torch to produce a neutral flame. Instead of helping me, they both laughed and made comments that suggested that my question was ridiculous.

A man seated behind a desk at the back of the shop overhead the conversation. He came forward and I couldn't help but notice that he was impeccably dressed in a pin-striped suit, a white shirt and a beautiful silk tie. He took off his jacket and hung it on the doorknob. He then rolled up his sleeves and tucked the tie into his shirt between the buttons.

He proceeded to roll out a welding setup. Using a flint striker, he ignited the torch and started to manipulate the valves to control the mix of the gases. The flame turned several different colors as he adjusted the ratio of oxygen to acetylene. After a few more seconds he smiled and held the torch up so I could see the flame. He said "Son, that's a neutral flame." I now knew what to look for when adjusting my torch and I thanked him for the demonstration.

I found out later that this gentleman was the owner and CEO of the supply company. This experience created a lasting impression on me that remains to this day. The CEO wasn't afraid to get his hands dirty and he was very knowledgeable regarding his product. Moreover, he was willing to spend some time offering his experience to a thirteen-year-old kid that had shown an interest in his trade.

The message he delivered that day was powerful and reached far beyond the neutral flame. He offered encouragement and a helping hand. He inspired me to continue tinkering and learning. I wanted to be like him. Those brief moments he spent with me shaped my priorities for years to come.

I extend a helping hand wherever I can to those who have an interest in learning from my experience. If you are not already doing this, I encourage you to look for those opportunities and pass along your expertise. I guarantee it will be a personally rewarding experience. For each contribution you make, you will be helping a less experienced employee gain a better footing as he advances along his career path.

In closing, I hope you enjoyed reading *Creating the Buy-in Magnet*. If you found the framework valuable, I achieved *my* goal. If you only found a few golden nuggets buried in the pages, perhaps it was still a worthwhile exercise.

Going forward I hope you have the courage to reach for those goals that were once considered unobtainable. If you made it this far, your leadership skills have the potential to deliver extraordinary results that can surpass the loftiest of goals. In the process you will inspire others. Good luck and remember to have fun in your pursuit of your future "Moon Shot" opportunities.

About the Author

Mr. Chapman spent over 40 years working in the Information Technology industry. His first job upon graduating from college was spent as an operations research analyst for a major bank in New England.

There, he provided valuable management information that was previously unobtainable. Much of his work was done on an IBM/370 mainframe computer running FORTRAN programs he developed using punched cards.

As a software developer, he worked for a startup mini-computer company, where he led a team of software engineers in designing, developing and implementing its corporate-wide order entry system.

He later moved into technical sales leadership and consulting roles for both venture capital-backed startups and established IT companies. He was a co-founder and CEO of a successful PC software startup company that focused on the food services industry.

He has always been an avid student of industry and has consistently placed a high value on continuous learning. His disciplined approach to leadership is the foundation of his success.

Mr. Chapman and his wife currently live on a lake in South Central Indiana. They raised two sons who are both currently employed in the IT industry. Mr. Chapman holds a BSBA in Finance from Northeastern University and an MBA in Entrepreneurship from Babson College.

www.ingramcontent.com/pod-product-compliance
Lightning Source LLC
Chambersburg PA
CBHW071213200326
41519CB00018B/5500